THE PUBLIC ECONOMY
OF METROPOLITAN AREAS

THE PUBLIC ECONOMY
OF METROPOLITAN AREAS

Robert L. Bish
University of Washington

Markham Series in Public Policy Analysis

Markham Publishing Company / Chicago

MARKHAM SERIES IN PUBLIC POLICY ANALYSIS

Julius Margolis and Aaron Wildavsky, Editors

PAPERBACK STANDARD BOOK NUMBER: 8410–0918–X

HARDBOUND STANDARD BOOK NUMBER: 8410–0917–1

LIBRARY OF CONGRESS CATALOG CARD NUMBER: 71–146015

COPYRIGHT © 1971 BY MARKHAM PUBLISHING COMPANY

ALL RIGHTS RESERVED

PRINTED IN U.S.A.

FOURTH PRINTING OCTOBER 1972

PREFACE

The objective of this work is to provide a method for explaining and understanding the structure and functioning of the public economy in metropolitan areas. The approach is to use a small set of assumptions common to economic analysis—methodological individualism, self-interest and individual rationality in the use of scarce resources—in a single paradigm to derive predictive hypotheses concerning economic activity not efficiently handled in private market exchange relationships. This method has been called non-market decision-making, the new political economy and the study of public choice by different scholars. I believe that this particular way of examining state and local government activity demonstrates the general applicability of economists' methods to political analysis.[1]

No claim is made that this is, or should be, the only way in which the public economy can be examined, but of several alternative theoretical concepts, it is one that has considerable utility.[2]

An application of the public choice approach to the state and local

[1] The subject matter of economics, like that of other disciplines, has no firm boundaries. Borderline material between traditional disciplines of economics and political science, such as this study, have been viewed as falling within the purview of economics because the analysis deals with choices in the allocation of scarce resources. For example, Lionel Robbins, in discussing legal and political frameworks, says: "There is an important sense in which the subject matter of political science can be conceived to come within the scope of our definition of economics. Systems of government, property relationships, and the like, can be conceived as the result of choice." (Lionel Robbins, *An Essay on the Nature and Significance of Economic Science* [2d ed.; London: Macmillan, 1935], p. 134).

[2] The social welfare function approach often used in economic analysis of political phenomena is specifically rejected in this study. Social welfare functions are (1) not usually empirically identifiable and, in fact, assume away the most difficult problem in nonmarket decision-making, the identification of the demands of the individuals; and (2) may bear no relation to actions of individuals rationally seeking their own interest in a limited-knowledge economy.

public economy is significant because state and local governmental units in the United States are increasingly important agents in allocating resources and dealing with domestic problems. All of the urban crises— transportation, housing, big city schools, environmental problems, etc.— require governmental and collective action for their solution. To the extent that a different way of thinking about these problems and their solutions facilitates their resolution, an academic study of this type can make a contribution both to the world of scholarship and to the solution of important public problems affecting citizens in their everyday lives.

I hope that this study will become part of the increasingly large body of literature using economic reasoning to analyze political phenomena. While the approach has a long intellectual history, it has been used explicitly by a large number of scholars only recently. Three major contributions were made during the 1950s: Robert A. Dahl and Charles E. Lindblom, *Politics, Economics and Welfare;*[3] William J. Baumol, *Welfare Economics and the Theory of the State;*[4] and Anthony Downs, *An Economic Theory of Democracy.*[5] During the 1960s, economic methodology was widely applied to analysis of non-market phenomena. The major monographs include: James M. Buchanan and Gordon Tullock, *The Calculus of Consent;*[6] Mancur Olson, *The Logic of Collective Action;*[7] Gordon Tullock, *The Politics of Bureaucracy*[8] and *The Organization of Inquiry;*[9] Duncan Black, *The Theory of Political Committees and Elections;*[10] William H. Riker, *The Theory of Political Coalitions;*[11] Charles E. Lindblom, *The Intelligence of Democracy;*[12] and R. L. Curry and L. L. Wade, *A Theory of Political Exchange: Economic Reasoning in Political Analysis.*[13] Many journal articles and conference presentations also reflect this trend, including William C. Mitchell's paper presented to the 1967 American Political Science Association meetings,

[3] (New York: Harper & Row, 1953.)
[4] (Cambridge, Mass.: Harvard University Press, 1965.)
[5] (New York: Harper & Row, 1957.)
[6] (Ann Arbor: University of Michigan Press, 1962.)
[7] (Cambridge, Mass.: Harvard University Press, 1965.)
[8] (Washington, D. C.: Public Affairs Press, 1965.)
[9] (Durham, N. C.: Duke University Press, 1966.)
[10] (Cambridge: Cambridge University Press, 1958.)
[11] (New Haven and London: Yale University Press, 1962.)
[12] (New York: Free Press, 1965.)
[13] (Englewood Cliffs, N. J.: Prentice-Hall, 1968.)

"The Shape of Political Theory to Come: From Political Sociology to Political Economy;"[14] many of James Buchanan's writings;[15] and two key articles treating metropolitan government, "The Organization of Government in Metropolitan Areas: A Theoretical Inquiry," by Vincent Ostrom, Charles Tiebout, and Robert Warren[16] and "A Municipal Services Market Model of Metropolitan Organization," by Robert Warren.[17] A new journal, *Public Choice,*[18] concentrates specifically on the application of economic methodology to political phenomena.

In addition to work on the borderline between economics and political science, some theoretical analyses within economics itself have facilitated many of the applications. While concepts of externalities and public goods are found in early writings by Wicksell, Pigou, Bowen, and Musgrave,[19] much of the current analysis relates directly to work done in the 1950s and 1960s by Paul A. Samuelson[20] on public goods, by R. H. Coase,[21] James M. Buchanan and William Craig Stubblebine[22] on externality theory, and the recent integrations in James Buchanan's *The Demand and Supply of Public Goods.*[23]

[14] Published in the *American Behavioral Scientist,* XI (November–December, 1967), 8–37.

[15] For example, see the articles contained in *Fiscal Theory and Political Economy* (Chapel Hill: University of North Carolina Press, 1960).

[16] *American Political Science Review,* LV (December 1961), 831–842.

[17] *Journal of the American Institute of Planners,* XXX (August, 1964), 193–204.

[18] Gordon Tullock, ed., Center for Studies in Public Choice, Virginia Polytechnic Institute, Blacksburg, Virginia.

[19] Knut Wicksell, "A New Principle of Just Taxation," in Richard A. Musgrave and Alan T. Peacock, eds., *Classics in the Theory of Public Finance* (New York: St. Martin's Press, 1967); A. C. Pigou, *The Economics of Welfare* (4th ed. [1932]; New York: St. Martin's Press, 1960); William H. Bowen, "The Interpretation of Voting and the Allocation of Economic Resources," *Quarterly Journal of Economics,* LVIII (November, 1943), 27–48; Richard A. Musgrave, "The Voluntary Exchange Theory of Public Economy," *Quarterly Journal of Economics,* LIII (February, 1939), 213–237.

[20] "The Pure Theory of Public Expenditure," *Review of Economics and Statistics,* XXXVI (November, 1954), 387–389; and "Diagrammatic Exposition of a Theory of Public Expenditure," *Review of Economics and Statistics,* XXXVII (November, 1955), 350–356.

[21] "The Problem of Social Cost," *The Journal of Law and Economics,* XXX (October, 1960), 1–44.

[22] "Externality," *Economica,* XXIX, N. S. No. 116 (November, 1962), 371–384.

[23] (Chicago: Rand McNally, 1968.)

I believe this study is organized in a logical way. Chapter 1 presents a perspective on the approach used in the study. It begins with data on the size, growth, and complexity of the state and local public economy and is followed by a discussion of basic assumptions and a clarification of the relationships between this methodology and the more traditional tenets of economics, political science, and public administration.

In the framework of this perspective, Chapter 2 summarizes recent developments in the theory of public goods, externalities, and collective action in order to draw conclusions concerning resource allocation problems not easily solved through voluntary market exchange. Chapter 3 presents a theoretical discussion of political, or nonvoluntary, associations to illustrate how such units may meet individuals' demands more efficiently than the market system. Chapters 2 and 3 present the basic theoretical framework within which examples from the American public economy will later be analyzed and compared.

Chapter 4 provides an overview of the structure and functioning of the Amercan public economy. It discusses the various types of political units and the coordinating mechanisms existing between and among political units, private organizations, and individual citizen-consumers. Chapter 5 analyzes two metropolitan area systems of government, those of Los Angeles County and Dade County, and Chapter 6 analyzes two public functions—education and air pollution control. Chapter 7 presents a summary of trends in the location of economic activities in metropolitan areas and an analysis of the resultant fiscal diversity. Analyses of the metropolitan area systems, the functional areas, and fiscal diversity are presented as examples of how the constructs developed in Chapters 2 and 3 help explain political phenomena, not as complete examinations of the phenomena in question.

Chapter 8 compares the model developed in this study with the traditional concepts of metropolitan political reform. The comparison explicitly defines the basis for differences in the conclusions regarding metropolitan area political systems and functional problems reached in this analysis, as contrasted with current analysis of these same phenomena using alternative theoretrical approaches. Finally, the concluding chapter, 9, will attempt to indicate some of the strengths and weaknesses of the approach presented here, including the plea customary in academic work for further application and research to indicate the fruitfulness of this approach to understanding and analyzing the state and local public economy in the United States.

This study was begun as a research paper for a joint Economics-Political Science seminar at Indiana University with Vincent Ostrom and Herbert Kiesling in 1967. Related research in public finance was also done for Louis Shere at that time. The first complete manuscript was written while supported by a summer salary award at the University of Washington during the summer of 1969. The Institute for Economic Research, the Urban and Regional Science Research Group, the Graduate School of Public Affairs, and the Graduate School at the University of Washington have all provided secretarial and research assistance support during the last year.

As with any piece of research, the ideas within it come from numerous sources, not all of which are easy to identify or remember. Both at Indiana and Washington, I benefited from discussion of the material in this study with students and faculty, and am grateful to Yoram Barzel, Albert Breton, Frank Doolittle, Marshall Enderby, Phillip Gregg, Gerald Meier, Nancy Neubert, Lynn Ostrom, Vincent Ostrom, Mark Sproule-Jones, Gordon Tullock, Robert Warren, Louis Weschler, Marc Whitney and Gilbert Wright for their comments and criticisms of the manuscript. I owe a special debt to Vincent Ostrom, not only for his assistance on this manuscript, but for the intellectual stimulation he has provided both during and after my graduate education.

R. L. B.
Seattle
October, 1970

CONTENTS

LIST OF FIGURES

Chapter 1

INTRODUCTION

THE STATE AND LOCAL PUBLIC ECONOMY

The state and local public economy is one of the faster growing sectors of the American economy, and most signs indicate that this trend will continue. State and local spending has been expanding as a proportion of Gross National Product and, in 1967, was 13.5 percent of GNP, or $106 billion out of a GNP of $785 billion. About 58 percent of all governmental non-defense spending was done by state and local governments. Of a work force of 77,347,000, approximately 7,454,000 persons were employed by state and local governments. Per capita state and local spending (perhaps the most meaningful indicator of magnitude for most people) was $536, or approximately $1620 per family—an amount equal to what the average American family paid for housing that year.[1]

Not only is a significant amount of economic resources allocated through the state and local public economy, but the structure is extremely complex; in 1967, state and local governments were comprised of over 81,000 political units. The number and types of governmental units are presented in Table 1.

While the total number of units has been decreasing, primarily because of school district consolidations, the number of municipalities has been slowly increasing (from 17,215 in 1957 to 18,048 in 1967) and the number of special districts has been increasing rather rapidly, from 14,424 in 1957 to 21,264 ten years later. As with the increased spending, it is reasonable to expect a continuation of current trends toward greater numbers of special districts and municipalities, offset to a degree by a

[1] Data from U.S. Bureau of the Census, *Census of Governments, 1967* (Washington, D.C.: U.S. Government Printing Office, 1967).

Table 1. Governmental Units in the United States

| Type of Government | Number of Units | | | | Percent Change 1952–67 |
	1952 [a]	1957 [a]	1962	1967	
Total	116,807	102,392	91,237	81,299	−30.4
States	50	50	50	50	.....
Local government units	116,756	102,341	91,186	81,248	−30.4
Counties	3,052	3,050	3,043	3,049	.....
Municipalities	16,807	17,215	18,000	18,048	7.3
Townships	17,702	17,198	17,142	17,105	−4.8
School districts	67,355	50,454	34,678	21,782	−67.6
Special districts	12,340	14,424	18,323	21,264	72.3

[a] Adjusted to include units in Alaska and Hawaii, which were reported separately prior to statehood of these areas in 1959.
Source: *Census of Governments.*

decrease in the number of rural school districts as urban-rural migration continues.

The state and local public economy is often described, but seldom is it analyzed as to relationships within and among government units or between them and the private sector of the economy. Unfortunately, most descriptions fail to grapple with the complex structure of the system, degenerating into calling state and local governmental organization, especially in metropolitan areas, "fractionated," "chaotic," "fragmented," "absurd," "historical accident," "a bewildering maze," "a crazy quilt of overlapping jurisdictions," and so on, and virtually always concluding with a recommendation for replacement of the existing systems with a simple, orderly, metropolitan wide governmental unit.[2] This kind of analysis is simply not adequate for understanding what is actually happening within and among the 81,000 local government units that continue to function in the economy and show little sign of disappearing in response to being designated as unintelligible by academicians and some observers of government. Some method of analysis is needed if the state and local public economy is to be understood and improved to solve the problems facing an industrialized and urbanized society.

[2] For a recent publication in this tradition, see the Committee for Economic Development, *Modernizing Local Government* (New York: CED, 1966), p. 11. Further studies drawing similar conclusions with a similar vocabulary are cited in Chapter 8.

During the past 200 years, economists have been relatively successful in explaining the organization and functioning of the private economy, a system much larger and even more complex than the state and local public economy. It is the methods of economics that this author believes will do much to provide an understanding of the organization and functioning of the public economy in the United States. While the following study will not conclusively prove this assertion, it will indicate that the complexity of the public economy may be a rational response to the complexity of the problems dealt with; hence, it cannot be condemned as chaotic out of hand.[3] In addition, the study will provide a significant start to further analysis within a rigorous framework.

ASSUMPTIONS

Deductive economic analysis usually starts with a statement and definition of basic assumptions, the format to be used in this analysis. One should, however, be aware that the seeming "reality" or "unreality" of the assumptions per se may not be an adequate guide for judging the usefulness of the model developed for predicting the outcomes of various actions.[4] The noneconomist who is unfamiliar with this approach may wish to look ahead to the analysis of government organization (Chapter 5), or of education and air pollution control (Chapter 6), to satisfy himself beforehand of the intuitive reasonableness of the application of the model. He should then be better able to see the significance of the theory-building material.

Four basic assumptions of economic analysis are common in the recent applications of economics to political phenomena. They will be discussed in detail at this point, being essential throughout this study. They are the assumptions of scarcity, methodological individualism, self-interest, and individual rationality in the use of scarce resources.

[3] Other scholars have reached this conclusion by different approaches. For example, urban planner William Alonso observes: "The chaos of which the critics complain, then, refers not to the lack of structure but to the difficulty of perceiving it; and the problem is not one of restructuring but one of making understanding easier." William Alonso, "Cities, Planners, and Urban Renewal," in James Q. Wilson, ed., *Urban Renewal* (Cambridge, Mass.: M.I.T. Press, 1966), p. 444.

[4] Milton Friedman, "The Methodology of Positive Economics," in *Essays in Positive Economics* (Chicago: University of Chicago Press, 1953).

Scarcity

Economics has been described as the science of scarcity,[5] because it studies the processes by which individuals allocate resources to satisfy individual desires. To date in human history, it appears that individuals desire more of many goods and services than is available. Thus, they have to pick and choose among goods and determine how much they wish to contribute in exchange for additional goods. This study focuses on the use of political organizations in the process of allocating goods and services. When goods and services are no longer scarce, I, as an economist, will be out of a job, but that will be quite all right as, by definition, I will be able to consume as many goods and services as I desire because they will no longer be scarce.

Methodological Individualism

Methodological individualism assumes the individual to be the basic unit of analysis for the purpose of this study.[6] This is not to imply that methodological individualism, as defined here, can be the only approach to the study of individual or collective behavior. Many studies have been made using organic conceptions of the state, of organizations, or aggregate constructs such as in macroeconomics (income, savings, consumption, investment), and useful analysis may flow from those concepts. Microeconomic analysis, however, has traditionally focused on the individual participants in the system, viewing the economy, society, and organizations as interactions intrinsic to individuals, not as something existing apart from those individuals. The individualistic postulate forms the basis for many of the public choice approach writings. Many of the implications of this assumption will become clear as the analysis proceeds.

[5] For example, Heinze Kohler chose the title *Economics: The Science of Scarcity* for his recent principles of economics text (Hinsdale, Illinois: Dryden Press, 1970).

[6] For a discussion of the difference between the ontological thesis ("the ultimate constituents of the social world are individual people") and the reductive thesis ("statements about social phenomena are deducible from psychological statements about human individuals"), see Ernest Nagel, *The Structure of Science* (New York: Harcourt, Brace & World, 1961), pp. 540–546. Only the ontological thesis comes within the methodological individualism defined above.

Self-Interest

The assumption here is that individuals undertake actions because they stand to benefit from them. This is a necessary assumption in analyzing an exchange relationship, even if the *quid pro quo* is love, admiration, or some other intangible. This does not mean that people are wholly selfish; obviously, individuals respond to more than material rewards or incentives and often act altruistically without accruing any apparent benefit. The major difficulty with this assumption is defining individual objectives so that predictions of rational behavior undertaken to achieve those objectives can be derived without becoming tautological; that is, by defining objectives derived only from analysis of the behavior. To avoid this problem, this study will stress only economic and political goals of individuals. Economic predictions based on the assumption of self-interest have been sufficiently accurate to justify the presumption that the principle will also yield good predictions when applied in non-market as well as market exchanges.

Individual Rationality

The assumption of individual rationality indicates simply that, in undertaking actions where choices are involved—and the choice may be one of whether or not to act—an individual will choose the course that he feels will give him the greatest satisfaction. The use of this assumption may be justified simply because it would be impossible to predict human behavior without it. The term individual rationality is used to avoid any confusion with organizational rationality. The Arrow impossibility theorem demonstrates the futility of expecting logical consistency from an organizational-choice process that combines individual preferences.[7] No generally accepted assumption in either economic or

[7] For example, if individual *I* prefers *A* to *B* and *B* to *C*, he logically prefers *A* to *C*. However, if we attempt to aggregate three individuals' preferences (*I* prefers *A* to *B* and *B* to *C*, *II* prefers *B* to *C* and *C* to *A*, and *III* prefers *C* to *A* and *A* to *B*) *A* is preferred to *B* by a majority, *B* is preferred to *C* by a majority, but *A* is *not* preferred to *C* by a majority. Thus, organizational (or community) rationality based on individual preferences is nonexistent even though each individual has rational preference orderings. The problem is compounded because no matter which outcome is selected, *A*, *B*, or *C*, a majority of individuals will always prefer a different outcome.

democratic theory indicates that organizational rationality in an organic sense should be expected where individuals are the units of analysis.

The four assumptions just stated, plus empirical observations on the nature of economic goods and services, can take one a long way in analyzing the structure and function of political actions, much as they have taken economists a long way in analyzing market activity.

RELATION TO ECONOMICS

While the assumptions of scarcity, methodological individualism, self-interest, and individual rationality are common to virtually all economic analysis, the approach developed here differs in many respects from other economic analyses. These differences are crucial to some of the conclusions reached in this study. Primarily, the distinction is the omission of certain other assumptions common in economic analysis: a high level of knowledge, the packageability of economic goods and services, a fixed legal structure, and an analysis of organizing modes in addition to the price system, including hierarchies, bargaining, voting, and recourse to adjudication. These considerations will be discussed in turn.

A high level of knowledge, sometimes referred to as "perfect knowledge," is a common assumption in economic analysis. This seems somewhat ironic as the problem of allocating resources in a society exists precisely as a single mind or a small group of minds cannot know all individual preferences and consequently, cannot maximize the efficient use of scarce resources. The major arguments supporting a decentralized price or market system rather than a completely planned system, where individual preferences are considered important, stem from the knowledge problem.[8] The presumption that an individual is likely to know his own situation best and that individual specialization will lead to innovation are at least as old as Adam Smith. Anthony Downs has analyzed some of the consequences of the cost of knowledge in *An Economic Theory of Democracy*.[9] The fact that knowledge is not avail-

[8] For a discussion of this point, see F. A. Hayek, "The Use of Knowledge in Society," *American Economic Review,* XXXV (September 1945), 519–530; and Armen A. Alchian, "Uncertainty, Evolution and Economic Theory," *Journal of Political Economy,* LVIII (June 1950), 211–221.

[9] Anthony Downs, *An Economic Theory of Democracy* (New York: Harper & Row, 1957), Part III.

able at zero cost will also play an important role in several of the normative and positive arguments made in the following analysis.

Another assumption often made for purposes of economic analysis, but omitted here, is the complete packageability of goods exchanged. A packageable good is one whose consumption, production or exchange affects no one except those directly involved. In our context, it is precisely because some goods have externalities, or are in the nature of public goods where one person's consumption does not detract from another's, that collective action is logically necessary to achieve an efficient allocation of scarce resources.[10]

In turn, the requirement of collective action to allocate efficiently nonpackageable goods leads us to bypass another assumption common to economic analysis: that of a fixed legal structure. Viewing the legal structure as constant is conceptually legitimate as long as economists are examining the effects of government activity on the private market or simply analyzing the effects of private activity on another private individual. However, much economic analysis is aimed at suggesting changes in the legal structure to facilitate the achievement of some objective. If the aim is to change the legal structure, to assume that it is constant for purposes of analysis would be self-defeating. A problem arises here, in that economists strongly argue that if one exogenous alteration is made in an economy its effects must be accounted for. One could apply the same reasoning to the legal system: one change may cause other changes, and it may be useful or necessary to examine consequences of initial changes. An excellent example of the application of economic methodology to the legal structure per se is Gordon Tullock's "General Standards: The Logic of Law and Ethics." [11] Tullock explains the evolution of the legal structure in the United States as deducible from the same assumptions used in this analysis. In a similar approach, this study will attempt to deduce a structure for the public economy rather than to start out with it as established. As will be illustrated in much of the rest of the work, public collective action raises consequences that set it apart from private market activity.

Consistently applying the assumptions of self-interest and individual rationality while omitting the assumption that perfect knowledge can be

[10] Externalities, public goods, and the logic of collective action will be explained fully in Chapter 2.

[11] Mimeographed (Houston, Tex.: Department of Economics and Political Science, Rice University, 1968).

accumulated by any single group or individual also will lead to conclusions for modification of private market economic activity different than those often drawn by economists who recommend such changes. A common approach in economics is to analyze a problem and suggest that the appointment of a monopolistic regulatory agency or coordinating board, analagous to an omniscient benevolent despot, will achieve the proper solution.[12] For example, after analyzing the northern California water industry, economists Bain, Caves and Margolis recommended "curtailing the discretionary powers of executives, executive departments, legislatures, and the bureaucratic agencies . . . and providing for an *independent* and *objective* appraisal of projects [italics mine]." [13] This kind of recommendation is at variance with market economics, in which regulation is imposed because consumers and businessmen have alternatives and are not dependent on the benevolence of a monopolist. In "Positive Economics, Welfare Economics, and Political Economy," [14] James M. Buchanan discusses the bifurcated-man behavioral assumption, where everyone seeks self-interest except the benevolent regulator. This issue will be discussed further in relation to the approaches applied by political science to the public economy and, more rigorously, in the discussion of constitutions and decision-making rules in Chapter 3. The important point is that this analysis applies logically consistent assumptions to individuals in the public as well as the private economy by assuming that the public sector is not composed of some benevolent mechanism that will make the proper adjustment in private market activity to achieve an efficient allocation of economic resources once the professional analyst (economist) adds knowledge to its other capabilities.

Economic analysis has been developed to its highest level of sophistication with regard to only one of several alternatives for the organization of economic activity—the market system—although the functioning of

[12] For an early recognition of this, see Knut Wicksell, "A New Principle of Just Taxation," in Richard A. Musgrave and Alan T. Peacock, eds., *Classics in the Theory of Public Finance* (New York: St. Martin's Press, 1967), pp. 82–87. For a more recent analysis, see Vincent Ostrom, "Water Resource Development: Some Problems in Economic and Political Analysis of Public Policy," in Austin Ranney, ed., *Political Science and Public Policy* (Chicago: Markham, 1968), pp. 134–141.

[13] Joe S. Bain, Richard E. Caves and Julius Margolis, *Northern California's Water Industry* (Baltimore: Johns Hopkins Press, 1966), p. 659.

[14] In *Fiscal Theory and Political Economy* (Chapel Hill: University of North Carolina Press, 1960), pp. 105–124.

hierarchies[15] and bargaining,[16] as supplements to the basic market system, have been given consideration. In an analysis of the public economy, alternatives to the market are relatively more important than in the private economy because the focus is on economic transactions of a type where individuals interacting in a market would not achieve efficient results. A discussion of some alternative organizing modes is presented by Dahl and Lindblom in *Politics, Economics and Welfare*.[17] A brief summary of these alternative organizing modes is presented here to point out their basic characteristics and to clarify usage of the terms throughout the rest of the analysis.

The Market System

An economic system must contain mechanisms for determining the composition of output, the allocation of scarce resources (labor, natural resources and capital) to produce the outputs, and the distribution of the output among consumers. A tremendous amount of information is required to carry out these functions. The price system is the primary basis for providing information and deciding economic issues in the American economy. For example, if a consumer desires a shirt, he goes to the store and purchases one. By making the purchase, he reveals that he is willing to pay a certain price. If there are more people willing to pay that price than there are shirts available, the price of shirts will be bid up and sellers and producers of shirts will realize increased profits. The profits will encourage more individuals to become sellers and producers of shirts. As output of shirts is increased, the demand will increase for resources used to produce shirts, such as cotton and sewing machines, and these prices are likely to be bid up as well. This will lead producers of cotton and sewing machines to demand more of the resources to produce their products; for example, land, fertilizer and cotton pickers for cotton production, and steel, tools, and skilled machinists to make more sewing machines. While the production of shirts is increasing and resources needed to produce them are being drawn into the shirt industry, production of some other goods and services,

---

[15] R. H. Coase, "The Nature of the Firm," *Economica*, N.S. IV (1937), 386–405; Richard M. Cyert and James G. March, *A Behavioral Theory of the Firm* (Englewood Cliffs, N.J.: Prentice-Hall, 1963).

[16] For a summary of work in this area, see Alan Coddington, *Theories of the Bargaining Process* (Chicago: Aldine, 1968).

[17] (New York: Harper & Row, 1953).

perhaps sweaters, will have to decrease because fewer resources will be available outside the shirt-making industry. An interesting and crucial aspect of this process is that the producer does not need to know why some purchaser wants more shirts, cotton, sewing machines, land, fertilizer, cotton pickers, steel, tools or skilled machinists. All he need know is that he can charge a higher price for an increased quantity of these products and labor than previously. The offer of a higher price indicates that consumers of these goods value them more than consumers of alternative products that could be produced from the same resources, and producers geared their production to reflect the change in consumer valuations.

Because an economic system is so complex that the knowledge of all consumer preferences and the efficient way to allocate resources to meet them is dispersed among many people, prices act to coordinate the separate actions of different people without recourse to separately designed (and usually costly) information systems required of hierarchical organization.

The model of the market system typically examined in economic analysis is that of perfect competition, where each buyer and seller is too small to influence the market price and a high level of knowledge exists. Full development of this model indicates that if none of the goods has external effects, the system will achieve an efficient allocation of resources to meet consumers' preferences.[18]

Hierarchies

Always recognized as part of a market system, hierarchical organization may be characterized as displaying employer-employee relationships where authority flows from the top downward (analagous to master-servant roles). Producing firms generally assume this form. Within hierarchical organizations, an individual takes the place of the price system for allocating resources and coordinating economic activity. Coase and Knight have argued that hierarchies supplant the price system for some resource allocation activities, because for combining factors of production into some products, coordination by central direction

[18] For a discussion of the market system, see any principles of economics text. For an effective analysis of efficiency conditions, see Francis M. Bator, "The Simple Analytics of Welfare Maximization," *American Economic Review*, XLVII (March 1957), 22–49.

is more efficient than the price system.[19] The size of an efficient hierarchy in a market system is limited to the point at which information and control loss within the hierarchy make it less efficient than the market system or alternative organizational forms.

Voting

Determining allocation either by direct vote or by electing a representative who will subsequently allocate resources represents an alternative to either the market system or hierarchical organization. In this respect, voting plays an obviously important role in the public sector, and the rationale behind its use instead of the price system or the hierarchical organization will be explored in Chapters 3 and 4.

Bargaining

Bargaining is interaction among individuals who have opportunities for increasing their welfare by exchanging resources over which they have discretion. Bargaining is not employed in pure competition because there are an infinite number of sellers and buyers who must simply accept the market price to enter into economic exchanges. Bargaining would also be unnecessary in a pure hierarchy because all authority would flow from the top down. However, the market system, voting, and hierarchical coordination are supplemented by bargaining as a coordinating device. Bargaining is often employed to determine wages and prices and to form political coalitions for the election of political representatives. Bargaining is frequent between political leaders and hierarchical leaders, within hierarchies, between members of a hierarchy and the customers it services, and between any number of interested participants in a decision-making process. Bargaining is not as easy to handle in simple models as are analyses of the market, hierarchies and voting; but it is of such frequency and importance that an analysis of the public economy must explicitly recognize the extent and importance of its use.

The market system, hierarchical organizations, voting and bargaining do not exhaust the potential mechanisms for allocating economic resources. Action may also be organized, for example, by recourse to legisla-

[19] Coase, "Nature of the Firm"; and Frank Knight, *Risk, Uncertainty and Profit* (London: London School of Economics Series of Reprints, No. 16, 1933).

tive or judicial processes (these might also be considered special cases of voting and bargaining), although these processes—especially the judicial—are usually costly and enlisted only after earlier accommodation attempts have failed.

Any examination of the public economy must give more consideration to the functioning of hierarchies, voting, and bargaining than would an analysis of the private economy. But, within the American constitutional and legal system, it is largely the nature of the goods to be produced that dictates the choice of organizational techniques alternative to the market system for the most efficient allocation of goods and services. Such choices, therefore, are rational by standards of economic analysis.

RELATION TO POLITICAL SCIENCE AND PUBLIC ADMINISTRATION

The approach taken in the new political economy has points of both agreement and disagreement with two closely related disciplines—political science and public administration—as their analysis is currently practiced. The major differences are related to two areas: basic methodology and the paradigm used.

Basic Methodology

The approach in this monograph is basically deductive; that is, the examination consists of a preliminary determination of the principal forces in operation (the assumptions) and deduction of their consequences under various conditions, followed by comparison of the deductions with empirical observation or testing to evaluate the theoretical concepts and constructions used. This technique, so common to economic analysis, is less widely used in political science. Political scientists have traditionally used the process of inductive generalization; that is, observing the real world and attempting to generalize from these observations. Both approaches have advantages and disadvantages; indeed, it is doubtful if either can be applied in its pure form, as even essentially deductive methods require induction for specifying initial assumptions. In actual practice, they tend to be mixed by most users. For example, Adam Smith's *Wealth of Nations*, often cited as the first example of economic analysis, uses essentially inductive reasoning to argue for a less controlled economy. On the other hand, *The Federalist Papers* contain long chains of deductive logic to explain the consequences of alternative constitutional arrangements, with a careful specification of the behavioral assumptions underlying the analysis.[20]

I do feel that the deductive approach has one advantage that has contributed greatly to the higher level of sophistication and prediction achieved by economics as a social science. It is the opportunity for continuity in method that enables new scholars to take up where their seniors have left off. As a result, analysis becomes a continuing and additive process. Because the assumptions and method are mutual, hypotheses tested in one area are thereby related to potential testing of hypotheses in others. Inductive generalization, on the other hand, opens the possibility that two observers will interpret the same phenomenon in different ways; indeed, for many political phenomena, an almost infinite variety of interpretations may be available. New insights may be gained by such divergence and erroneous concepts may not last as long; but a continuing academic inquiry faces almost insuperable difficulties when scholars are unable to agree even on common definitions for important words and concepts in their working vocabularies.[21] Economics has made its progress not because many of its phenomena are quantifiable (indeed, no numbers whatsoever need be attached to an analysis of the functioning of an economic system), but because of the powerful deductive methods employed. Primarily, the new political economy is an extension of essentially deductive methods to political phenomena.

Alternative Paradigms

Two polar conceptions, or paradigms, of political science theory are useful for comparison with the approach taken here, as this analysis is very much a part of one of them and differs extremely from the other paradigm employed especially in relation to public administration. This

[20] For an analysis of *The Federalist Papers* in this regard, see Vincent Ostrom, "The Political Theory of the Compound Republic: An Essay on the Federalist Papers," mimeographed (Bloomington: Department of Government, Indiana University).

[21] For a discussion of these aspects of theory construction, see Abraham Kaplan, *The Conduct of Inquiry: Methodology for Behavioral Science* (San Francisco: Chandler, 1964), pp. 269–272, 302–306.

difference has been explored recently by Braybrooke, Lindblom, Ostrom and others.[22]

The American tradition in public administration as illustrated in the writings of Woodrow Wilson, Frank Goodnow, Leonard White, and Luther Gulick adheres to one mutual and logically consistent paradigm.[23] These writers separate politics from administration and attempt to identify the center of power and its relation to a linear system of bureaucratic authority. Their approach, termed "synoptic" by Braybrooke and Lindblom, resembles Plato's, who was concerned with getting the "wisdom" and the "power" located at the same place—preferably in the same person, the Philosopher King. An appropriate characterization of this paradigm is found in Dwight Waldo's *The Administrative State*:[24]

> The Philosopher-King union of all wisdom and all power in one or a few as a short cut to Utopia—there is no more familiar pattern in the history of political theory than this. One enlightened chief administrator with adequate power is all that is necessary, and so much easier to secure than hundreds of enlightened legislators or millions of enlightened citizens.

Underlying assumptions of the synoptic model are very similar to those made by some economists who recommend omniscient benevolent despot solutions: that the individual at the top of the controlling political hierarchy will be both knowledgeable and benevolent in his direction of public activities.

Advocates of the synoptic model and American tradition of public administration generally fail to recognize that coordination within the public sector may be achieved by nonhierarchical means. Thus, their

---

[22] David Braybrooke and Charles E. Lindblom, *A Strategy of Decision* (New York: Free Press, 1963); Charles E. Lindblom, *The Intelligence of Democracy* (New York: Free Press, 1965); and Vincent Ostrom, "The Politics of Administration," mimeographed (Bloomington: Department of Government, Indiana University).

[23] Woodrow Wilson, "The Study of Administration," *Political Science Quarterly*, II (March, 1887), 197–223; Frank J. Goodnow, *Politics and Administration* (New York: Macmillan, 1900); Leonard D. White, *Introduction to the Study of Public Administration* (4th ed.; New York: Macmillan, 1955); Luther Gulick, "Notes on the Theory of Organization," in Luther Gulick and L. Urwick, eds., *Papers on the Science of Administration* (New York: Institute of Public Administration, Columbia University, 1937).

[24] (New York: Ronald Press, 1948), p. 38.

conclusions are inapposite for a system that regularly employs a variety of coordinating devices.

A paradigm that differs from the synoptic model is found in both the old classics, such as the works of Madison and de Tocqueville,[25] and in recent works that use the public choice approach, of which this study is a part. Madison, in Papers 37 through 51 of *The Federalist,* argues that authority should be dispersed, rather than concentrated. In fact, Madison said that "the accumulation of all powers, legislative, executive, and judiciary, in the same hands, whether of one, a few, or many, and whether hereditary, self-appointed, or elective, may justly be pronounced the very definition of tyranny." [26] Recent works of Charles Lindblom,[27] Morton Grodzins,[28] and Vincent Ostrom[29] emphasize that the American public economy is structured to avoid the concentration of power in a single center. Not even the executive branch of the Federal Government possesses a single power center.[30] Public choice approach economists concur with classical theorists in viewing the American public economy as an equilibrium system, not a linear system. Indeed, the deductive analysis in this study will emphasize that if the assumptions used here have a normative value, the equilibrium system is the rational way to organize for the achievement of individual welfare.

A NOTE ON POSITIVE AND NORMATIVE ANALYSIS

Both economics and political science face problems in separating positive and normative analysis. This study is no exception. The assumptions used in this analysis were chosen because of their long, successful record in economic analysis and their recent illuminating applications to politi-

[25] Alexander Hamilton, John Jay, and James Madison, *The Federalist* (New York: The Modern Library, n.d.); Alexis de Tocqueville, *Democracy in America* ed. Phillips Bradley (New York: Knopf, 1945).

[26] *The Federalist,* p. 313.

[27] Lindblom, *Intelligence of Democracy.*

[28] Morton Grodzins, *The American System* (Chicago: Rand McNally, 1966).

[29] Vincent Ostrom, "Operational Federalism: Organization for the provision of Public Services in the American Federal System," *Public Choice,* VII (Spring 1969), 1–17.

[30] Aaron Wildavsky, *The Politics of the Budgetary Process* (Boston and Toronto: Little, Brown, 1964).

cal phenomena. Not much conscious thought was given to their potential normative qualities. However, since beginning the examination of political phenomena in this manner, I have become increasingly convinced that these assumptions provide an understanding of the American public economy because they closely resemble the postulates underlying the constitutional structure of the United States and acknowledge the value of the individual in the Western intellectual and cultural tradition.

The relationship between positive and normative analysis is explicitly illustrated by a comparison of the assumptions underlying the strongly normative *Federalist Papers* and the United States Constitution and the assumptions used in this analysis. In the *Federalist Papers,* the arguments and long deductive analysis specify the assumptions that (1) the individual, not the state, must be the unit of analysis and criteria for evaluation—this is identical to the assumption of methodological-individualism used in this analysis; (2) because man will seek his own interest, the institutional structure must be so structured that public officials keep check on each other and that monopoly positions are to be avoided because of the difficulty of controlling individuals holding the monopoly—this is parallel with the position argued in this study that self-interest will motivate the individual in *both* private and public positions; and (3) men are *capable* of rationally designing their own affairs to produce desired results—a stronger assumption than the one used in this analysis: that men will *try* to achieve their objectives. The entire process of formulating a constitution was seen as man's attempt to create a more desirable institutional structure to order his affairs and further his aims.

The normative arguments in *The Federalist Papers* flowing from these assumptions accorded with the long tradition of Western thought that holds the individual important in his own right and views political or collective organizations as servants of the group of individuals. This thesis is totally opposite to the concept, carried to the extreme in German romantic philosophy and in Naziism, that individuals exist for the sake of promoting some organic statehood.

Although the aim of this study is to abide by positive analysis, many of its conclusions may prove useful to those who believe its assumptions are desirable normative goals and wish to discover recommendations for improving the present structure and functioning of the American state and local public economy. For those who seek to promote other aspects of behavior, the analysis provides an understanding of the current situation—prerequisite to more effective implementation of their own objectives.[31]

[31] For a discussion of normative judgments related to the individualistic approach, see David Braybrooke, *Three Tests for Democracy* (New York: Random House, 1968), and James M. Buchanan and Gordon Tullock, *The Calculus of Consent* (Ann Arbor: University of Michigan Press, 1962), Appendix 1.

Chapter 2

EXTERNALITIES, PUBLIC GOODS, AND COLLECTIVE ACTION

INTRODUCTION

Recent developments in the economic theory of externalities, public goods, and collective action greatly facilitate an analysis of the public economy. They form the building blocks for the public choice approach to the analysis of political phenomena. The purpose of this chapter is to explain these concepts, as they are basic to the analysis of the state and local public economy. All of the theoretical implications of each concept cannot be explored in this presentation; references are provided to more advanced treatment of some of the issues elsewhere in the literature.

EXTERNALITIES

Externalities are the results of an economic action that affect parties not directly involved in the transaction. The effects may be either beneficial, referred to as positive externalities or spillovers, or harmful, referred to as negative externalities or spillovers. An example of a positive externality is the pleasure (or lack of displeasure) that A derives from the attractive landscaping of an industrial site that he must pass each day. On the other hand, the odor that emanates from a nearby pulp mill and A must tolerate is a negative externality. To identify an externality is not, in itself, to indicate that something should be done about it—perhaps, through some type of private bargaining or through public or collective action. Buchanan and Stubblebine[1] have provided a set of definitions that enable one to classify externalities specifically with regard to individual incentives for changing the externality situation.

Nonrelevant Externalities

Nonrelevant externalities are those that are too unimportant to stimulate a desire for action. Decorating your automobile with floral decals may incite approval or disapproval, but it is unlikely that any viewers of the flowered automobile will want to do anything about it. Nonrelevant externalities are also called "trivial"; the main purpose of this classification is to eliminate unimportant cases from analysis.

Relevant Externalities

Relevant externalities, on the contrary, exert a strong enough influence to incite individuals to action, either to reduce the effects of a negative externality or to increase the effects of a positive externality. Faced with relevant externalities, the affected party is willing to forego something to change the level of the externality; that is, the demand for change is an effective demand. A common example of a negative relevant externality is the restriction of an individual's view by untrimmed trees in a neighbor's yard when the person whose view is blocked is willing to bear some of the costs of tree trimming. Flowered automobiles would generate positive relevant externalities if individuals were willing to pay for the privilege of viewing them. Conversely, the flowers would produce negative relevant externalities if viewers were willing to pay to have the flowers removed.

Pareto-Relevant Externalities

Pareto-relevant externalities are a special case of relevant externalities. Pareto-relevant externalities exist when the maximum that affected parties are willing to pay exceeds the minimum the generator of the externality is willing to accept to alter his action. Such externalities, therefore, provide an opportunity for action that can make both the

---

[1] James M. Buchanan and William Craig Stubblebine, "Externality," *Economica*, XXIX, N.S. No. 116 (November 1962), 371–384.

generator of the externality and the affected individual better off or, at minimum, one of the parties is better off while the other is no worse off.[2]

For example, if a viewer who receives great satisfaction from observing flowers on automobiles were willing to pay car owners enough to induce them to put on more flowers, the bedecked automobiles would be producing Pareto-relevant externalities. On the other hand, if a distressed viewer were willing to sufficiently compensate owners of flowered automobiles to induce them to remove the flowers, gains from trade could be made under such conditions of negative Pareto-relevant externalities.

Where the cost of removing a relevant externality exceeds the benefits of its removal it is called Pareto-irrelevant. For example, if an individual is unwilling to pay the fee necessary to have view-blocking trees trimmed, he would be better off to leave the trees untrimmed; thus, net gains from removing the externality are not possible.

Marginal and Nonmarginal Externalities

Marginal externalities occur when a small change in the level of activity generating the externality alters the magnitude of its effects. Under nonmarginal externalities, an all-or-none situation exists over some range of changes in the level of the externality. For example, if adding additional flowers to an already flowered car increases the external effects or if additional trimming of view-blocking trees decreases the external effects, the additional flowers or additional trimming would be producing marginal changes in the externality and could be termed marginal externalities. If adding ten flowers to an automobile that was already decorated with twenty did not change the level of the viewer's satisfaction or trimming more branches did not improve the view, however, the change would be nonmarginal.

Externalities generally are classifiable in three categories: they can be either positive or negative; non-relevant or relevant (with relevant externalities divided between Pareto-relevant and non-Pareto relevant); and marginal or nonmarginal. The importance of these classifications for economic analysis will be brought out in the following sections.

[2] Designation of externality situations where gains for both parties are possible as "Pareto-relevant" is taken from the definition of a "Pareto optimum" economic situation. A Pareto optimum is a situation where it is not possible to make anyone better off without making at least one person worse off by any changes in the allocation of resources.

Efficient Control of Externalities

In an economic efficiency sense, nonrelevant or non-Pareto relevant externalities are not important whether positive or negative, marginal or nonmarginal. The reasons they are not economically important in themselves is definitional: nonrelevant externalities produce no demand for change; non-Pareto relevant externalities generate an insufficient demand to provide an opportunity for at least one party to improve his position and no one is deprived in the process. That is, the maximum the affected party is willing to pay for a change in the level of the externality is less than the minimum the individual generating the externality is willing to accept to change his actions. Economic transactions can be expected to occur only when both parties can improve their positions, or at least only when no one is placed in a worse position, and only Pareto-relevant externalities offer this opportunity.

The welfare implications of an externality situation can be illustrated with simple demand-supply analysis, such as that presented in Figure 2-1, which shows a situation in which an activity of individual A generates negative externalities for individual B.[3]

In Figure 2-1, marginal net benefits from undertaking the activity are illustrated by a downward sloping line (JM), reflecting decreasing marginal net benefits to A over this range of activity.[4] The costs borne by B from A's activity (the value of the negative externality) are indicated by an upward sloping line (ON), illustrating that as the level of activity increases over this range, B bears increasing marginal costs.

If A had the right to undertake production and there were no interaction between B and A, A would undertake the activity at level M, where his net benefits would be maximized. A's net benefits would equal the area under the marginal net benefits curve, OJM. At level of activity M, individual B would be bearing total costs equal to the area under his marginal costs curve, ONM. At any output level greater than O, B has an effective demand (is willing to pay a positive price) to have A's activity reduced; thus, the negative external effects of A's activity on B are relevant. However, at activity levels up to L, the marginal amount of B's damages, shown by the marginal cost curve, is less than A's

---

[3] For a graphical analysis of all the types of externalities see Buchanan and Stubblebine, "Externality," p. 379, Figure 2.

[4] It is assumed that the activity is subject to the law of diminishing returns.

marginal net benefits, so no gain can be made from trade and the externality is non-Pareto relevant. At levels of activity greater than K, B's marginal damages exceed A's marginal net benefits, so gains from trade are possible because B is willing to pay A to restrict his activity to

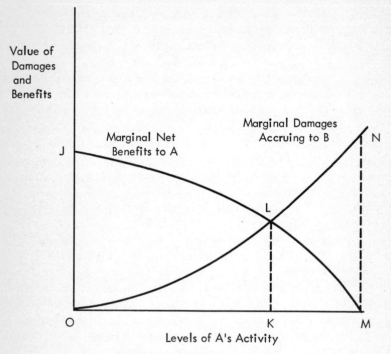

Figure 2-1. Two-Party Externality

level K, an amount greater than the benefits A would receive by expanding activity beyond K. The negative externality at levels greater than K is Pareto-relevant. Activity level K, the point at which all Pareto-relevant externalities have been removed, can be shown to be the level of activity generating the greatest amount of net benefits for A and B; i.e., the sum of A's gain minus B's loss is maximized. At level K, benefits are equal to $OJLK$, and costs are equal to OLK. At any level of output less than K, an expansion of activity would increase benefits faster than the increase in costs because marginal net benefits are greater than marginal costs at every point. At any level of activity greater than K, on the other hand, benefits from additional units are less than costs from additional units, so that reductions in the level of activity would reduce costs more than the reduction in benefits.

How would output level K be achieved? [5] If A and B can bargain with one another without incurring any decision-making costs[6] and the income effects from the property right allocations are too small to affect the valuation of costs and benefits from the externality, output K will be achieved whether A has the right to produce or B has the right not to incur costs generated by A. If A has an unlimited right to produce, at any level of activity greater than K, B will be willing to pay A a sum greater than the net benefits A could receive by continuing the activity at that level to reduce the activity. The precise amount of compensation is not determinable. To reduce the activity from M to K, B would be willing to pay a maximum just less than $KLNM$. A would be willing to reduce activity from M to K for any amount slightly greater than KLM. Thus, the net gains, equal to LNM, would be available for division between A and B in some indeterminate manner.

Now, if B had the right to prevent A's imposing costs on B, B could simply prevent A from undertaking any activity. However, at level K, the amount of potential gain to A is equal to $OJLK$, and A would therefore be willing to pay B an amount slightly less than $OJLK$ to gain permission to undertake activity level K. B, on the other hand, would be willing to accept a minimum slightly greater than OLK, the amount of his damage, to permit A to undertake activity level K. The net gains to both A and B from undertaking activity level K are equal to $OJLK$ minus OLK, OJL, so A and B could divide the net gains (OJL) in some manner. Thus, it does not matter whether A has the right to undertake the activity or B has the right to prevent A from imposing costs on him; both will find it to their advantage for the activity to reach level K as long as bargaining costs are zero. If bargaining costs are positive but the amount is less than potential gains from trade, we would expect bargaining to take place and the activity level to ap-

[5] For a discussion of legal cases, see R. H. Coase, "The Problem of Social Cost," *The Journal of Law and Economics,* III (October 1960), 1–44.

[6] Decision-making costs, also called bargaining costs, are all of the costs borne by individuals in reaching an agreement regarding the allocation or exchange of economic resources. They include the value of time and effort engaged in bargaining as well as any direct outlays. If bargaining costs are zero, it is generally assumed in economic analysis that individuals will continue to bargain until all gains from economic exchange have been exhausted and a Pareto optimal allocation of resources is achieved.

proach K, but perhaps not to reach it. This is because as activity level approaches K, potential gains from trade will diminish and eventually, bargaining will cease as its cost exceeds potential additional gain.

The existence of externalities has often been presented as a justification for governmental action to supplement private market activity. However, a third party (representative government) could not help to achieve economic welfare beyond enforcing property rights in the above example.[7] Under the assumptions used in the above example, it would be predicted that Pareto-relevant externalities will be eliminated strictly through private market activity. However, the crucial assumptions are (1) that one or the other party has a legal right to do something within a system of enforced law and property rights, and (2) that decision-making costs are zero. These conditions are likely to be violated (1) if property rights are not carefully specified (for example, does a city have the right to dump sewage into a river, and if so, how much, or do downstream water users have the right to prevent the upstream city's polluting the water?) or (2) if a large number of individuals are involved since decision-making costs are likely to increase in proportion to the number of people involved. What if A's activity affected one hundred B's instead of just one? The problem of uncertain property rights is likely to increase bargaining costs[8] whether two or two thousand individuals are involved and, conversely, bargaining costs are likely to increase parallel with an increase in the number of participants whether or not property rights are carefully specified. Bargaining costs are likely to be highest when both these factors are involved, and many of the most pressing environmental problems facing the United States today are of precisely this type. The concepts of various types of externalities are important, but they must be supplemented with additional theoretical constructs directed toward the critical problems of large numbers of

[7] In fact, where bargaining is possible between the two parties, the intervention by a third party may actually result in nonoptimal solutions to the problem. Buchanan and Stubblebine, "Externality."

[8] If property rights are uncertain, the potential gains or losses to each party are larger, justifying an increased output of bargaining effort. For instance, in Figure 2-1 A could potentially gain OJM plus a share of LNM if he obtains the property right (or B could avoid a loss of ONM and gain a share of OJL). If property rights are certain, only the shares of OJL or LNM can be negotiated, rather than the larger amounts, OJM or ONM. James M. Buchanan and Gordon Tullock, *The Calculus of Consent* (Ann Arbor: University of Michigan Press, 1962), p. 103.

participants, uncertain property rights, and high decision-making costs to effectively analyze the subnational public economy.

The following discussion of public goods and collective action will treat issues of high decision-making costs related to a large number of participants. Property rights and techniques to reduce decision-making costs through political action are treated in Chapter 3, "Political Organization."

PUBLIC GOODS

Public goods[9] are goods that can be consumed by one person without diminishing the consumption of the same good by another *and* where exclusion of potential consumers is not feasible. For example, national defense is a service that is available to every citizen and an increase in population does not cause a decrease in services for original citizens. The qualifying clause differentiates this case from the situation where exclusion is feasible because the good can be packaged and sold on the private market. An example of this type of good is a movie that is shown in a theater. Nonpayers can easily be excluded, but up to the point where crowding occurs, one person's consumption does not detract from another's. Examples of public goods include national defense services, flood control, and the legal structure. Some public goods, such as foul-smelling industrial odors, are often referred to as "public bads." This use of the term "public" relates only to the nature of the good and has nothing to do with the nature of the producer, whether it is a public government or a private firm. The public aspect relates only to the form of consumption of the goods.

Because like externalities, public goods are a general class of phe-

---

[9] Terminology of authors varies. The terms "social goods" and "collective goods" also are used to describe "public goods" as defined here. The basic analyses of public goods are found in: William H. Bowen, "Interpretation of Voting and the Allocation of Economic Resources," *Quarterly Journal of Economics,* LVIII (November 1943), 27–48; Richard A. Musgrave, "The Voluntary Exchange Theory of Public Economy," *Quarterly Journal of Economics,* LIII (February 1939), 213–237; and Paul A. Samuelson, "The Pure Theory of Public Expenditure," *Review of Economics and Statistics,* XXXVI (November 1954), 387–389, and "Diagrammatic Exposition of a Theory of Public Expenditure," *Review of Economics and Statistics,* XXXVII (November 1955), 350–356.

nomena, several distinctions drawn on the basis of other characteristics may increase the usefulness of the concept. Two of these distinctions are whether a public good is equally available for everyone's consumption and whether an individual has a choice with regard to consumption if the good is produced. There are very few pure public goods, so a classification based on additional characteristics is useful for further analysis.[10]

Equal Availability

Some goods are more equally available for consumption than others. For example, an air raid siren relays the same information to everyone within range. The national defense system provides the same general services for everyone in the country. On the other hand, freeways and flood control measures are available for all (since the principle of exclusion does not apply), but some individuals will find them much more accessible and, hence, valuable, than others. The example of the air raid siren service also illustrates that equal availability may be related very directly to a specific geographic area—all within hearing distance of the siren enjoy equal utility from an available public good. Those beyond hearing distance do not have that public good available to them; thus, spatial relationships may determine the question of equal availability. Flood control and freeways are generally considered to be unequally available because location within a small area plays an important role.

Choice

A second useful distinction hinges on whether an individual has a choice concerning consumption of the good. Some public goods offer the individual no choice—the air raid siren will be heard by all individuals within its range. On the other hand, use of some public goods that are not exclusionary is completely within the discretion of the in-

[10] For an example of a classification scheme for public goods followed by an analysis of efficient methods for their provision see Elinor Ostrom, "On the Variety of Potential Public Goods," mimeographed (Bloomington: Indiana University). Several examples in the following analysis are taken from this paper.

dividual. Local parks and freeways, for example, are available for all, but one can choose whether he wants to use them. A much discussed case of a public good where free choice is crucial is called "option demand." [11] This is an effective demand to make something available for the individual's future use. Option demand is important for some all-or-none decisions; for instance, where contributions from potential users are necessary to maintain transit service or to provide national parks. If an individual is willing to pay for their future availability, it is the option for use, not the actual use, that is the public good. The option that each person has does not diminish its existence for another.

Very few economic goods are pure types, as between private or public, or in the case of public goods, as between equal or unequal consumption or between no freedom of choice versus complete freedom of choice in consumption. Also, public goods provided in one area (say, a municipality) may generate externalities for individuals in other areas. The concepts of public goods and externalities are closely related, and any externality accruing to a large number of people may be accruing in the nature of a public good. For instance, the odor of a pulp mill may be an externality (it accrues to individuals who do not participate in transactions concerning the pulp mill's production) and the odor may accrue as a public good, or bad (anyone in the area will consume the odor without detracting from someone else's consumption). As a happier example, the provision of a free regional park by a municipality will be not only a public good (up to the point of crowding or increased maintenance costs) for its residents, but is likely to provide a positive externality, also available as a public good, to individuals residing outside of the municipality's boundaries.

Local governments face many boundary problems related to public goods and externalities. Different kinds of public goods have different spatial aspects or boundaries (for instance, the divergent areas served by a neighborhood park and by national defense), and the difference bears importantly on a determination of the level of government able to provide the good most efficiently. The boundary problems of public goods and externalities are analyzed in Chapters 3 and 4.

[11] Burton A. Weisbrod, "Collective-Consumption Services of Individual-Consumption Goods," *Quarterly Journal of Economics*, LXXVIII (August 1964), 471–477.

Efficient Provision of Public Goods

It is easy to define an optimal level of provision for a public good. It is less easy to identify the optimum provision of any single public good empirically. In this section, a definition of the optimal provision within a single area or for a small group of people will be examined. In Chapter 3, the problems of externalities resulting from the provision of public goods for a single group will be studied.

The optimum level of consumption of any good is defined as the level where the individual's marginal evaluation is equal to the marginal cost of the good. Thus, for a packageable good, an individual simply buys additional quantities until his marginal evaluation is equal to the price that will reflect the marginal cost of the good—assuming that there is a perfectly functioning competitive economy and zero externalities of production or consumption—and the optimum level of consumption will be achieved.[12] Public goods present some special problems. First, if one individual provides a public good, other individuals may consume the good without paying for it—simply treating it as a positive externality generated by someone else's action. This would make no difference to the individual who purchases the good, as he would be expected to purchase to the level where his marginal evaluation is equal to his marginal cost; however, for the group as a whole, the level of provision of the public good is likely to be below the optimum level unless some kind of collective or cooperative activity is taken. An optimum level of provision can be achieved only if each individual contributes an amount equal to his marginal evaluation for the last unit of the good produced and some contribute to pay for the intramarginal units. The optimum level and marginal prices are illustrated in Figure 2-2. Since price is assumed to be constant, the marginal cost curve is

[12] The logic behind marginal analysis is quite simple but an explanation may be useful for noneconomists. It is generally assumed that additional units of a good provide decreasing amounts of satisfaction from its consumption. At the equilibrium level of consumption, the satisfaction from the last unit (that is, marginal utility) will be equal to the price of the good. This is because at any lower consumption level, an individual would be better off by expanding consumption because the additional satisfaction would be greater than the price, and at any consumption level greater than the equilibrium level, an individual would be better off by reducing consumption because he would be giving up units for which satisfaction was less than price. The equilibrium level is, of course, the level at which the individual is best off and cannot make net gains by changing.

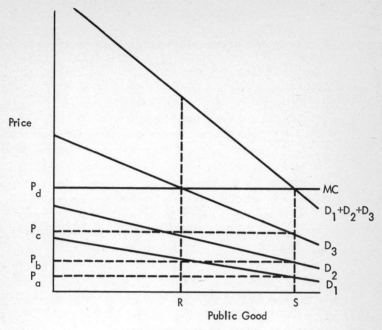

Figure 2-2. Public Good

horizontal. Demand curves are drawn sloping downward in keeping with the law of diminishing returns. The graph illustrates that aggregation of the demand for a public good by several individuals is different from that which would apply for a private good. With the latter, demand curves must be added horizontally because for each individual the total amount of the good must be expanded or his consumption will directly reduce another individual's. With public goods, demands are added vertically—and the summed demand $(D_1 + D_2 + D_3)$ represents the total amount all three individuals are willing to pay to achieve a particular output that they can simultaneously consume. In Figure 2-2, individual 3 would be willing to provide output R at price P_d for his own use. If he did this, individuals 1 and 2 would be able to consume R without making any payments. However, if decision-making costs are zero, there are net gains to be made if individuals 1, 2, and 3 get together and provide output S, where the sum of their marginal evaluations is equal to the marginal cost. At output S, D_1 is willing to contribute P_a for the marginal unit and some amount less than

his total benefits (the area under his demand curve up to S) as his
contribution toward payment for the intramarginal units. Individual 2
would be willing to contribute P_b and individual 3 would donate P_c
for the marginal unit plus some amount less than total benefits for the
intramarginal units. At output S, total costs would be equal to S times
P_d (or the area under the MC curve), and total benefits would be
equal to the area under the summed demand curve $(D_1 + D_2 + D_3)$
up to S; at this point, the total net benefits are maximized because at
any lower output, increases would add more to consumer benefits than
to total costs, and at any higher output, reductions would lower costs
more than the reduction in consumer benefits.

In general, under conditions of *zero-cost decision-making* and constant costs,[13] we would expect individuals in small groups to cooperate
to provide optimum levels of a public good. If bargaining is a positive
cost process, output S may be approached but probably will not be
reached, and additional decision-making will cease when its costs exceed
potential gains (and potential gains decline as they approach S). With
large groups, decision-making costs may be quite high, leading to under-
consumption, or perhaps to no consumption, of a public good. The problems related to group size are treated in the next section of this chapter,
in which the concepts of public goods are directly related to a theory
of collective action. Mancur Olson has carried the development of this
approach farthest, and the presentation here is taken largely from his
work, *The Logic of Collective Action: Public Goods and the Theory
of Groups*.[14]

COLLECTIVE ACTION

An analysis of externalities and public goods indicates that group size
is an important factor in the ability of individuals in a group to achieve
an efficient level of public goods consumption, because the larger the

[13] The problem is somewhat more complicated if the assumption of constant costs is dropped. For an analysis of this situation, see Robert L. Bish
and Patrick D. O'Donoghue, "A Neglected Issue in Public Goods Theory:
The Monopsony Problem," *The Journal of Political Economy*, LXXVIII
(November–December, 1970), 1367–1371.

[14] Olson, *The Logic of Collective Action: Public Goods and the Theory
of Groups* (Cambridge, Mass.: Harvard University Press, 1965), ch. 1.

group, the higher the decision-making costs are likely to be. This may be the case, but group size may also radically affect the participants' decisions as to the utility of bargaining at all. In small groups, individuals are likely to realize their interdependence and to be aware of potential benefits from cooperative action. In large groups, however, individuals may not sense their interdependence, and even if a potential for gains from cooperative action is recognized, they may still find it in their individual interest *not* to enter into the cooperative action. Olson has provided useful conceptual terminology for different size groups, which will be adopted for this analysis.

Privileged Groups

Privileged groups are small enough so that one member would be willing to make some provision of a public good alone, without the cooperation of other potential or actual consumers. Figure 2-2 illustrates a three-person privileged group where individual 3 would provide output R without cooperation. The single individual's provision of the public good is likely to be suboptimal for the group as a whole, as is level R in Figure 2-2, but the few individuals involved are likely to recognize the potential to be gained by cooperating to expand output to S.

Intermediate Groups

In an intermediate group, a single individual would not provide the public good without cooperation, but the group is small enough so that the demands of a few individuals are sufficient to make them realize the potential that could be gained by cooperating. Over the range of intermediate group sizes between privileged groups and the next group size (latent groups), the larger the group, the less any individual will feel that his own group-oriented activity can achieve and the less incentive he will have for group-oriented action. The demand and supply relations for an intermediate group are illustrated in Figure 2-3. In Figure 2-3, a cooperation between individuals 1 and 2, the two individuals with the highest level of demand, would be sufficient to provide output T of the public good. An optimal output level, U, where the sum of all demands is equal to the marginal cost, could be achieved only with the cooperation of additional individuals.

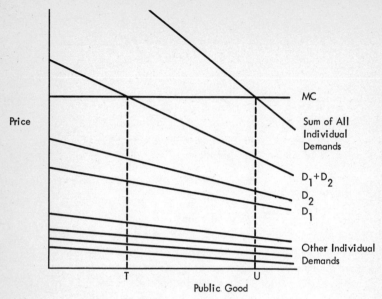

Figure 2-3. Public Good—Intermediate Group

Latent Groups

Latent groups are so large that a single individual's contribution makes no perceptible difference to the burden or benefit of other members of the group or to his own consumption of the public good. The demand-supply conditions for a latent group are illustrated in Figure 2-4, where any single demand is extremely small relative to total demand or cost.

The difference between privileged or intermediate groups and latent groups is not only in size per se, but in the incentives for individual action. In the small groups, obvious interdependence affords an incentive for cooperation to obtain the public good. In contrast, the person in a latent group lacks incentive to bargain or to enter into a cooperative agreement because he can see that his action will be ineffective. He also knows that if the public good is provided, he may as well be a free rider, consuming the public good as long as others provide it, because his contribution will make no perceptible difference in the level of supply. One would predict that unless some positive or negative incentive

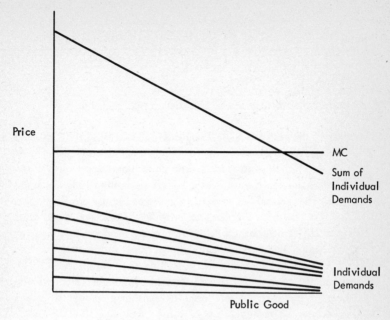

Figure 2-4. Public Good—Latent Group

is offered in addition to the public good, latent group members will not be provided with the public good. For example, would national defense be provided in the absence of sanctions for not paying taxes, or could labor unions afford to lobby for governmental legislation or bargain for higher wages if membership were completely voluntary but benefits accrued to members and nonmembers alike? Olson analyzes several private and quasi-private organizations, including labor unions, the Farm Bureau, and the American Medical Association, that provide services for their members in the nature of public goods and concludes that all use some selective private reward or sanction system in addition to the public goods to assure the public good activity.[15]

The latent group problem is also referred to as the free rider problem because its members consume public goods that others have provided. This is likely to be perfectly rational from the standpoint of the individual who considers that any contribution he might make would be greater than the potential increase in benefits. This problem is ampli-

[15] Olson, *Logic of Collective Action,* ch. 6.

fied if decision-making costs are positive and must be included when comparing total costs of the public good and benefits from its consumption.

SUMMARY

Discussion of the concepts of externalities, public goods, and collective action indicates where problems are likely to arise if all economic activity is to take place among individuals through voluntary exchange. Problems of externalities are most serious when decision-making costs are high because the externalities accrue to a group or because property rights are not clearly specified. Problems of providing public goods are most serious when a latent group is involved, because members of the latent group lack individual incentives to entice them into a bargained or cooperative relationship. Externalities accruing to a group are likely to be in the nature of a public good (occurring simultaneously with the production of the privately produced or consumed good); thus, the group aspects of externality problems can be treated within the public goods framework relating to collective action. In summary, then, problems of economic efficiency within a voluntary exchange economy are most likely to arise where latent groups and unclearly specified property rights are involved either or both of which may make the decision-making costs greater than the net benefits individuals think they can achieve through voluntary action. Techniques for reducing decision-making costs are treated explicitly in Chapter 3, "Political Organization."

Chapter 3

POLITICAL ORGANIZATION

INTRODUCTION

The examination of externalities, public goods, and collective action in the last chapter led to the conclusion that problems of collective action are likely to be related to high costs of decision-making among large voluntary groups, often complicated by unclearly specified property rights. In this chapter, techniques for reducing the decision-making costs of large groups will be examined. These techniques will then be related to the size and scope of political units efficiently organized to satisfy individual demands in the public economy. The first part of this analysis draws heavily on Buchanan's and Tullock's *The Calculus of Consent: The Logical Foundations of Constitutional Democracy*.[1]

SOCIAL INTERACTION COSTS

Social interaction costs are defined as the costs of cooperation between or among individuals for their mutual benefit. In a purely voluntary exchange economy, these would consist solely of decision-making costs. In a politicized economy, some of the costs are likely to be political externalities. Both of these concepts will be defined in turn.

Decision-Making Costs

Obtaining two or more individuals' agreement to undertake an economic action gives rise to decision-making costs, which include the

[1] James Buchanan and Gordon Tullock, *The Calculus of Consent: The Logical Foundations of Constitutional Democracy* (Ann Arbor: University of Michigan Press, 1962).

value of time, effort, and any direct outlays going into the bargaining process. Such costs are likely to increase with (1) the size of the group, and/or (2) increased opportunities for strategic bargaining. Increased costs attributable to group size are simply the result of having to obtain agreement among an increasingly large number of people. Decision-making costs within latent groups, for instance, are likely to be very high because each individual sees the cost of contributing to group aims without seeing that his individual contribution will have any effect on providing a public good. Increased opportunities for strategic bargaining are also likely to raise decision-making costs. Strategic bargaining is possible when an individual is in a position to hold back his support and demand a relatively large share of any benefits before he will participate in the group action; the strength of his bargaining power will, of course, depend on the importance of his cooperation to the rest of the group. Strategic bargaining costs are vitally affected by the size of the potential surplus: the larger the surplus, the greater the incentive for an individual to devote increased time to strategic bargaining in an attempt to obtain a larger share for himself.[2] For the group as a whole, however, bargaining over the division of a surplus is a zero-sum situation (that is, the group as a whole makes no net gains) since one individual's increased share is directly offset by another's decreased share. Thus, decision-making costs to divide the surplus are a net loss to the group. Strategic bargaining, in addition to increasing costs related to time and effort, may lead to stalemate situations where no action is undertaken. In this case, all decision-making costs are net losses because there are no compensatory benefits from undertaking the joint action over which the bargaining occurred.

Decision-making costs can be illustrated by an upward-sloping line on a graph relating total decision-making costs to the number of members in the group. Figure 3-1 illustrates the relationships. Costs are shown on the vertical axis, the number of individuals on the horizontal axis. Decision-making costs are zero where only one person is involved, positive where two are involved, and increase as the number of individuals increases.

Social interaction costs, equal to decision-making costs when voluntary consent is required for action, contain a second important element

---

[2] An economic "surplus" is a benefit *above the minimum* required to induce action.

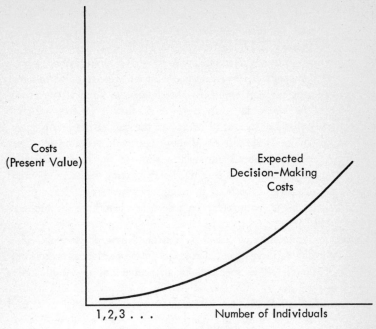

Figure 3-1. Decision-Making Costs

when the voluntary consent conditions are dropped. This second element has been called political externality costs.

Political Externality Costs

In Chapter 2, negative externalities were defined as costs imposed on an individual as a by-product of someone else's economic action. Political externality costs are similarly imposed by actions of others, but they occur when a political organization coerces an individual into participating in economic action with which he does not agree. If the local school board decides to increase the budget for education by raising local taxes, all residents will bear the costs whether or not they agreed with the school board's decision. Those who disagree can be said to have borne "costs" (that is, increased taxes) imposed on them through the political process by the actions of others. In general, political externality costs will be a decreasing function of the proportion of the members of the political unit required to agree before action by the unit is taken. For example, if any single person could commit the political unit to undertake public works financed from general taxation, each random individual member of the unit could be forced to bear very high political externality costs, paying for projects from which he receives no benefit. If 50 percent of the group were required to agree before action by the unit could be taken, potential political externality costs would be lower, but still positive, because a random member would have a 50-50 chance of belonging to the half of the group agreeing on the action. If 90 percent of the group were required to agree, political externalities would diminish because of the high probability that any member would be part of the motivating majority. Political externality costs would be zero if unanimity were required for group action, in which case political action would be identical with voluntary group action.[3]

Political externality costs can be illustrated by a downward-sloping line on a graph relating potential costs to the proportion of a group required to commit all its members to an action. Figure 3-2 illustrates these relationships.

Potential costs of political externalities could be expected to depend on the issues the political unit has authority to decide, as well as on the proportion of members required to commit the group to action. For example, when a political unit is limited to relatively low decision-making costs and, hence, can impose only very low taxes, potential costs to an individual will be relatively low even if he does not benefit from the tax-financed action. On the other hand, if the political unit is empowered to undertake actions which could potentially deprive an individual of all his property or even of his life, political externalities are potentially extremely high.

To determine the least costly decision-making rule for a group of individuals, it is necessary to compare the present value[4] of both

---

[3] This is obviously a *status-quo*-oriented approach that is justified in building positive models because the objective of this study is to predict (1) the logic of the present political structure and (2) changes from the *status quo*. Normative implications are not drawn.

[4] Present-value comparisons are necessary in selecting decision-making rules for *future* actions so that the problem of comparing costs and benefits accruing at different periods of time is accounted for. For a good discussion of the logic underlying present-value comparisons, see Jack Hirshleifer, James C. DeHaven and Jerome W. Milliman, *Water Supply* (Chicago: University of Chicago Press, 1960), ch. VI.

decision-making costs and political externality costs. Political externality costs can be substituted for decision-making costs when members of a group agree in advance to drop the requirement for voluntary consent in undertaking group action. It may, therefore, be possible to reduce the

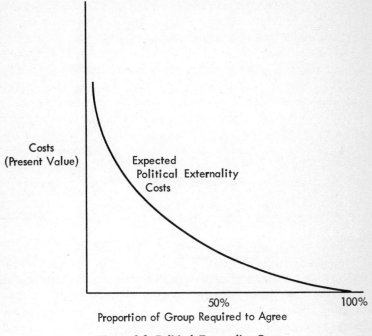

Costs
(Present Value)

Expected
Political Externality
Costs

50%   100%
Proportion of Group Required to Agree

Figure 3-2. Political Externality Costs

social interaction costs by entering into such an agreement. Such an agreement sets ground rules upon which future action can be based and is analogous to a political group's constitution.

The relationships between decision-making costs and political externality costs are illustrated in Figure 3-3. In the situation illustrated in Figure 3-3, the shape of the curves representing decision-making costs and political externality costs are such that the lowest potential social interaction costs are attainable at a decision-making rule of approval by slightly over 50 percent of the group. This indicates that the potential costs for the individual illustrated are such that the reduction in decision-making costs from a 100 per cent decision-making rule to

55 percent decision-making rule is greater than the potential increase in political externality costs over that range for the potential future undertakings of this group. Thus, it would be rational for that individual voluntarily to commit himself in advance to cooperate whenever 55 percent of the group agreed on an undertaking.

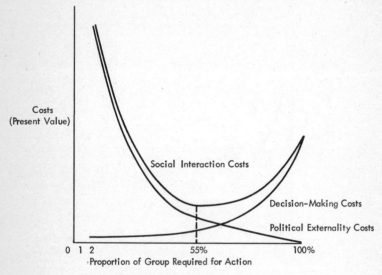

Figure 3-3. Social Interaction Costs

It is also possible that cost curves could indicate a very small proportion of the group as the least costly decision-making rule (which would imply that decision-making costs were high relative to potential political externality costs); or the least costly decision-making rule might be shown to be very high, perhaps reaching *unanimity* (implying extremely high potential political externality costs relative to decision-making costs). These two hypothetical situations are illustrated in Figures 3-4 and 3-5. Figure 3-4 illustrates a situation where decision-making costs are high relative to political externality costs, and Figure 3-5 demonstrates the converse situation.

Whenever individuals in a group have a demand for a public good, including the removal of negative externalities that accrue in the nature of public goods, they may find that organizing into a coercive group is the most efficient procedure, so decisions binding on all members can be made with less than unanimous consent. Coercive groups are designated as political groups in this analysis. Most actual political organizations share the capacity, through a decision-making rule of less than unanimity, to commit members of the unit (citizens) to some economic

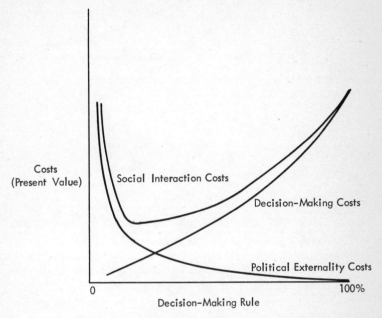

Costs
(Present Value)

Social Interaction Costs

Decision-Making Costs

Political Externality Costs

0   100%

Decision-Making Rule

Figure 3-4. Social Interaction Costs: Low Rule Optimal

action. The formation of political groups is justified for many functions strictly on a basis of economic efficiency.

The unanimity criterion may still be appropriate for reaching agreements on decision-making rules, referred to by Buchanan and Tullock[5] as constitutional decisions. The application of such a criterion to constitutional decision-making rules indicates that no one would expect net losses from entering into an agreement where he could be committed to action without his consent; each would presumably expect positive gains to accrue from participation.[6]

[5] Buchanan and Tullock, *Calculus of Consent*, pp. 63–84.

[6] This approach of agreement on decision-making rules is very similar to that of John Rawls as discussed in "Justice as Fairness," *Philosophical Review*, 67 (April, 1958), 164–194.

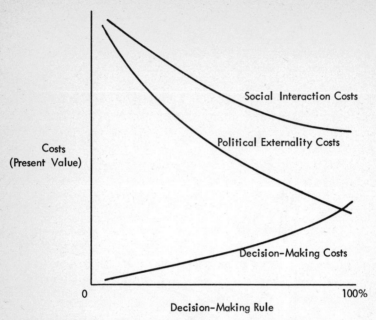

Figure 3-5. Social Interaction Costs: High Rule Optimal

The discussion of alternative decision-making rules in this analysis has assumed a framework within which individuals, at least a number sufficient to obtain the required consensus to undertake action, consider the potential actions to be taken and express their views, perhaps by voting. It is obvious from casual observation that most political units do not solicit day-to-day participation by members of the group on all actions undertaken, but delegate authority to individuals responsible, to a greater or lesser degree, to the citizens bearing the costs and receiving the benefits of the unit's activities.

A discussion of participation, delegation, and leadership will indicate the economic efficiency of such relationships. This will be followed by a specific examination of conditions determining the optimum size and scope of political organizations in an economy.

PARTICIPATION, DELEGATION, AND LEADERSHIP

Interaction with a political group involves costs for a citizen, even though the costs may be less than those he would have to incur if he were to undertake voluntary collective action. Individuals must obtain information about issues and find some mechanism for making their preferences known. The model developed in the first part of this chapter is essentially based on direct citizen-organization relationships, perhaps with citizen preferences being determined by voting on all issues and action being undertaken when the number necessary to pass the vote approve the action. The process of voting on every issue, however, is likely to incur costs that, for several reasons, might exceed potential benefits for any individual citizen.[7] First, the voter is only one of many, and the larger the group the less impact his single vote will have. Thus, the individual must weigh the probability of his vote determining the outcome against the cost of voting. Second, the voter has to make some estimate of how much he will benefit or lose if the issue he is to vote on is accepted or rejected. It may be quite rational for individuals to consider alternatives to the high costs of direct voting on every issue, to reduce social interaction costs.

One method of reducing the costs of making decisions for the provision of private goods and services is through delegation.[8] Individuals consult specialists who assume responsibility in making their decisions in medicine, law, horticulture, interior decorating, and many other activities. Similarly, individuals may find it rational to delegate decisions on public goods and services, the main difference being that, in the public sector, the delegate is commonly chosen by election rather than through direct contract between two individuals. Voting for an individual to make choices on a single issue would be very similar to voting on the issue itself; for example, when we vote for electors who, in turn, cast ballots for a presidential nominee, the intercession of the electors is usually inconsequential to the outcome. However, the advantage of electing a delegate lies in selecting one person to represent us on many issues, so that one choice—the vote for a delegate—substitutes for many separate decisions on each issue as it comes up.

The reduction of costs attainable by electing a delegate to act on multiple issues introduces an additional problem into the individual's calculations. That is, when several candidates offer themselves as potential delegates, the individual voter may not find one who agrees with

[7] Anthony Downs, *An Economic Theory of Democracy* (New York: Harper & Row, 1957), ch. XIV, pp. 260–276.

[8] Gordon Tullock, "Federalism: Problems of Scale," *Public Choice,* VI (Spring 1969), 26.

him on every issue, but will discover that he must weigh the positions of each candidate on several issues and vote for the one who comes closest to his own views or who, on the basis of past experience, campaign oratory, or amenability to influence, is judged likely to come closest to his own choice on future issues. This problem of choosing one delegate to represent the voter on a variety of issues complicates the problem of measuring the impact of a single vote on the final public policy outputs emerging from delegate interaction. The issue becomes still more complex when delegate interaction may, in turn, result in further delegation, such as to subcommitteemen, or to administrators selected by the delegates.

Competition for political positions has the potential for providing the electorate with more than just a delegate to represent their views on previously identified issues. In a quest for votes, delegates have an incentive to seek new solutions to issues and to identify potential public goods for latent groups. Downs has credited political party competition in the United States with both increasing the ability of voters to predict where a delegate will stand on an issue and creating organizations designed to translate voter demands into public policy outputs to supplement the political units themselves.[9] Initiative on the part of delegates, potential delegates, or party functionaries on behalf of delegates may be characterized as leadership, and especially creative individuals serving in those roles are often designated as political "entrepreneurs," acting in the public arena rather than in the private marketplace.[10]

The interaction between participants and public policy outcomes is extremely important and is, indeed, the focus of many studies. The important point in this analysis is that delegates and potential delegate competition form a mechanism for reducing the social interaction costs of individuals in their attempts to articulate demands for public goods. Three aspects of the system are especially significant: first, the delegation process *per se* permits voters to substitute one decision for many decisions; second, in an attempt to gain votes, the competitors for delegate positions produce low-cost information for voter use; and third, active

[9] Downs, *Economic Theory,* pp. 14–141, 226–227.

[10] For a discussion of the role of political entrepreneurs in collective action analysis, see Richard E. Wagner, "Pressure Groups and Political Entrepreneurs," in Gordon Tullock, ed., *Papers on Non-Market Decision Making* (Charlottesville, Va.: Thomas Jefferson Center for Political Economy, 1966), pp. 161–170; and Robert H. Salisbury, "An Exchange Theory of Interest Groups," *Midwest Journal of Political Science,* XIII (February 1969), 1–32.

political contenders have an incentive beyond that of any noncompeting group member to seek *new* solutions to problems and to identify latent demands that are not being met.

Despite the complexities involved in the translation of individual demands into public goods outputs through the political process, it is possible to construct political organizations that articulate the demands of individuals into the economic structure for production of public goods and services. The efficacy with which this happens in any particular governmental unit is an empirical question requiring detailed research beyond the scope of this study. Despite the complexity, some implications can be drawn concerning the size and scope of political units *most likely* efficiently to meet citizen demands for goods and services not adequately met in the private market. In the next section, I will attempt to draw such conclusions in the abstract. Chapter 4 will lend somewhat more support to the abstract formulations in its analysis of the types of political units that have been created specifically to handle problems of public goods and externalities.

THE SIZE AND SCOPE OF POLITICAL UNITS

The efficiency with which citizen demands are articulated and public goods and services provided can best be analyzed from the standpoint of two basic concepts of economic analysis: demand and supply. This approach is often ignored in analysis of the structure and functioning of the public economy, usually because of the implicit assumption that the political unit through which demands are articulated is also the production unit supplying the good. In addition, in discussing the "optimum size and scope of political units," most analyses have concentrated only on supply conditions, such as economies of scale and government boundary spillover problems.[11]

[11] For example, see Alan Williams, "The Optimal Provision of Public Goods in a System of Local Government," *Journal of Political Economy,* LXXIV (February 1966), 18–33; William C. Brainard and F. Trenery Dolbear, Jr., "The Possibility of Oversupply of Local 'Public' Goods: A Critical Note," *Journal of Political Economy,* LXXV (February 1967), 86–90; Alan Williams, "The Possibility of Oversupply of Public Goods: A Rejoinder," *Journal of Political Economy,* LXXV (February 1967), 91–92; Geoffrey Brennan, "The Optimal Provision of Public Goods: A Comment," *Journal of Political Economy,* LXXVII (March/April 1969), 237–241.

Because both demand and supply conditions about efficient organization in the public sector must be considered before any conclusions can be drawn, we begin with an analysis of demand conditions consistent with the position that political units are created to help articulate and meet the demands of individuals for goods and services not efficiently handled in private market exchange.

Demand

Chapter 2 analyzed the problems of articulating or identifying individual demands for controlling externalities and the provision of public goods and services. The first section of this chapter provided the rationale, from an individual's point of view, for forming a political unit to articulate demand in order to reduce the decision-making costs of purely voluntary activity. The discussion on participation, delegation, and leadership has briefly touched additional mechanisms for reducing decision-making costs in the same respect. The efficiency of these techniques for reducing costs is an empirical question, but some a priori considerations indicating that the political structure does reduce decision-making costs below those that would be incurred in voluntary economic transactions were discussed. An analysis of three additional considerations, however, will permit us to draw some conclusions regarding the most efficient size and scope of political units for articulating individual demands.

Heterogeneity of Individual Preferences. Individuals generally have different demands for goods and services, and this is true for public as well as for private goods. No one expects all families, even with identical incomes, to spend their incomes identically. Some buy suburban garden space and a lot of transportation, while others buy yardless apartments and little transportation; some buy steak, charcoal, and broilers; others buy steak and the services of cooks, waiters, and dishwashers. The same families exhibit equally diverse tastes for public goods. Some prefer public parks and others prefer private recreation areas; some prefer high-quality education, others prefer different goods and services. There is no reason to expect that all members of any given group want exactly the same output of either public or private goods.

Diverse preferences are not generally a problem with private packageable goods. Each individual or family buys the goods it desires and only market relationships are affected. However, a problem arises with regard to demands for public goods that must be provided collectively. In most cases, a single level must be provided for all families in an area, and no individual is able to adjust his consumption level to precisely meet his demand at the tax price he must pay. He usually does not have the option of adjusting his tax price to equal the marginal valuation of the level of public good supplied, because that would be a direct reintroduction of the free-rider problem that was removed by the collectivization of the activity in the first place. Figure 3-6 illustrates the problem of the inflexibility of adjustment of either tax price or quantity of public goods provision consumed. In Figure 3-6, an individual (D) with demand SE is pictured as paying tax price OT per unit for provision of a public good. His optimum supply level would be output B, where D's marginal valuation would be equal to his marginal tax price. At that output, he would maximize consumer surplus (TSG),[12] which is equal to the area under his demand curve $(OSGB)$ minus his outlay $(OTGB)$. However, if the public good were provided at level A and at price T, individual D would obtain less than his optimal amount. At output A, his consumer surplus has been reduced to $TSLF$, and he incurs a welfare loss equal to FLG in relation to his optimal position (ignoring any costs of achieving the optimum). On the other hand, it is possible that output C of the public good will be provided, in which case individual D incurs a welfare loss of GHJ relative to the optimum, his actual consumer surplus being equal to TSG minus GHJ. (However, at the output of public goods of either A or C, individual D is better off than he would have been with no provision of the public good. In that case, his welfare loss would have equaled the entire consumer surplus of TSG.)

If, in Figure 3-6 individual D sees no connection between his taxes and the provision of the public good, he may vocally demand output E of the public good, where his marginal valuation of zero equals his apparent tax price. It is possible that there is an output of the public good, perhaps E, where, in fact, an individual is made *worse off* by the provision of the public good. At output E, individual D would be paying an amount equal to $OTKE$, while receiving benefits equal to

[12] Consumers' surplus is the difference between total benefits from consumption of a good (equal to the area under the demand curve) and the cost of purchasing the good (equal to price times quantity). Equilibrium is achieved where the consumers' surplus is greatest.

OSE. If the area *GKE* is greater than area *TSG, D's* position would be worse than if no public good production had been undertaken. Thus, it is possible for public goods production to make individuals worse off,

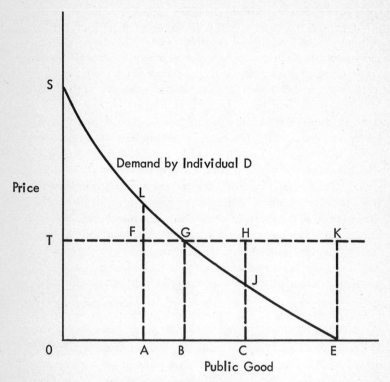

Figure 3-6. Public Goods and Price

as well as to improve their level of welfare. Thus far, the general conclusion from the analysis is simply that the closer the level of production of public goods comes to meeting an individual's demand (at a given tax price), the better off he will be.

The level of public goods provision is assumed to be most efficiently determined through the political process, as discussed in the first two parts of this chapter. If the process works relatively well, with a majority-rule basis, the level of production is likely to approach the median level of combined individual demands.[13] Any individual would achieve the highest level of satisfaction if his tastes were identical to the median tastes in the political unit of which he forms a part; thus, he has two ways of influencing his level of consumption of public goods. First, he can participate in the political process so that his tastes are taken into consideration in determining the level of output; second, he can choose to reside in a political unit where the provision of public goods is closest to his preference level. If many individuals made residential choices with public goods considerations in mind, groups of people with similar tastes would congregate together.[14] Figures 3-7 and 3-8 illustrate the demand characteristics of political communities comprising people with homogeneous and heterogeneous tastes respectively. If everyone's tax price were equal and the consumer's surpluses of all individuals were totaled, one would find a relatively higher level of satisfaction in the homogeneous community.

The most efficient use of economic resources takes place when individual demands can be exactly accommodated, as in a purely private-good market. When it is necessary to combine individual demands for a public good, the most efficient political unit for articulating the demand is a relatively homogeneous one, the limiting case being one where all individuals in the unit have identical demands. Apparently, individuals with similar tastes for public goods live in the same neighborhoods.[15]

An example of diverse demands that are not being as effectively articulated as possible can be illustrated by looking at a geographic area with six hypothetical neighborhoods, all in the same political structure. Within these six neighborhoods, two have relatively high demands for

[13] For an analysis of voting and public goods outputs, see Gordon Tullock, *Toward a Mathematics of Politics* (Ann Arbor: University of Michigan Press, 1967), chs. III and IV.

[14] Charles M. Tiebout, "A Pure Theory of Local Expenditures," *Journal of Political Economy*, LXIV (October 1956), 416–424.

[15] James W. Simmons, "Changing Residence in the City: A Review of Intraurban Mobility," *Geographical Review*, LXIII (October 1968), 622–651; Edgar Chasteen, "Who Favors Public Accommodations? Demographic Analysis," *Sociological Quarterly*, IX (Summer 1968), 309–317; John F. Speight, "Community Homogeneity and Consensus on Leadership," *Sociological Quarterly*, IX (Summer 1968), 387–396; Irving S. Foladare, "The Effect of Neighborhood on Voting Behavior," *Political Science Quarterly*, LXXXIII (December 1968), 516–529.

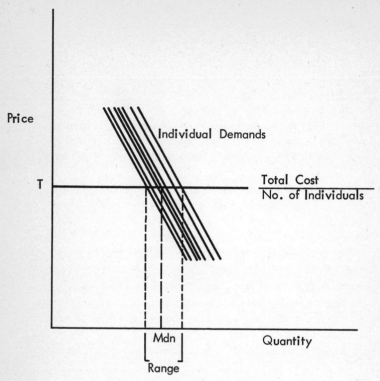

Figure 3-7. Homogeneous Group

neighborhood parks (those densely populated neighborhoods within the center of the city); two have relatively homogeneous demands for a median level of neighborhood parks (those older sections of the city containing single-family homes with extremely small yards); and two have relatively low demands for neighborhood parks (those newer residential sections with large-yard single-family dwellings). If demand were aggregated within the same political structure, the probable output would be a median provision of neighborhood parks throughout the city, which would fully satisfy only the two areas having median-level demand. Residents of the high-demand neighborhoods would be willing to pay more to get more parks, and the low-demand neighborhoods would feel they were paying for unwanted parks. If each neighborhood could articulate its own demands, the high- and low-demand neighborhoods would both find themselves better off, and the median-level

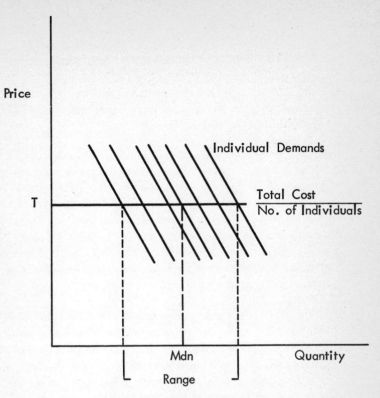

Figure 3-8. Heterogeneous Group

neighborhood would find its situation unchanged. Thus, independent articulation of demand by neighborhoods of people with similar tastes would lead to a higher level of satisfaction.[16] If people with heterogeneous tastes were spread completely and equally over the larger political unit, however, the articulation of a neighborhood's demand would not result in either a reduction or an increase of welfare.

The heterogeneity or homogeneity of populations within political units is also likely to affect the social interaction costs of political decisions. Both decision-making costs and potential political externalities are likely to be lower in a group of people with similar tastes. There-

[16] James R. Pennock, "Federal and Unitary Government—Disharmony and Frustration," *Behavioral Science,* IV (April 1959), 147–157; and Yoram Barzel, "Two Propositions on the Optimum Level of Producing Collective Goods," *Public Choice,* VI (Spring 1969), 31–37.

fore, a group of homogeneous individuals will be able to achieve a higher level of welfare in the provision of public goods because each individual's demand will be closer to the median level, and the social interaction costs will be lower than in heteregeneous groups. Relatively homogeneous groups, then, would be expected to exhibit a higher level of collective activity because a larger number of collective actions will achieve net benefits in excess of social interaction costs.[17]

Setup Costs and Existing Units. In addition to heterogeneity or homogeneity of groups, a second major influence helps to determine boundaries of a political unit for articulation of demand for provision of a public good. This is the high initial cost of reaching agreement on a constitutional structure and decision-making rules to assure less costly decision-making in the future. Because of the high setup costs, it may be more efficient for individuals to use an existing political structure to articulate demand even if the boundaries of the existing unit are not quite as efficiently drawn as would be true of a group organized for a specific purpose.

The political leaders of existing units may also be the first to recognize the existence of a latent group for which they can provide a public good, even if the boundaries of the latent group are not precisely those of the existing political unit. Thus, the existing political system will influence the boundaries for handling future public goods problems. Despite a failure to reach optimum boundaries in articulating demand, the existing political units may prove to be the most efficient tool to employ, especially if benefits can be gained from combining the demands for a variety of public goods within the same political unit.

The Multiplicity of Public Goods. There are many potential and existing public goods. Individual voters would find it extremely difficult to keep track of what is going on if a separate unit were maintained for implementing each demand for a separate good, even if the voter only elected a delegate to act for him on providing each good (rather than vote on every issue). Therefore, voter decision-making costs are likely to be reduced when the demands for several public goods are set forth through the same political unit. For instance, it may be quite efficient to delegate control over the provision of street sweeping, road maintenance, and highway construction to the same political unit within

[17] Buchanan and Tullock, *Calculus of Consent,* p. 115.

an area and control over the provision of elementary, secondary, and post-high school education to another.[18]

While every aggregation will reduce an individual's ability to articulate his own particular preference on each of the issues involved, combining some functions in the same unit should result in sufficient savings in decision-making costs to more than offset the loss of precise demand stipulation. However, since efficiency of aggregation is likely to be higher among individuals with similar preferences, there is still further reason for individuals desiring the same goals to group together in attempting to attain a variety of public goods.

The discussion of homogeneity, existing units, and the multiplicity of public goods has been related only to the articulation of demand, with no reference to supply conditions relating to public goods. We can conclude a priori that implementation of demand will be lower in cost and will meet individual preferences more closely in homogeneous groups than in heterogeneous groups; thus, to the extent that efficient demand articulation is important to individuals, we will see individuals with similar tastes living together, and perhaps expressing preferences quite different from residents of other neighborhoods, which have relatively homogeneous demands indigenous to their own circumstances.

Supply

The supply conditions for a public good also enter into the consideration of the efficient size and scope of political units. However, the major supply condition generally analyzed in relation to the optimum size of government units—economy of scale—is, under many conditions, not relevant to the question of the optimum size of any political unit. Instead, the supply conditions that are important in that determination concern (1) boundary problems of spillovers to other groups of people, and (2) the technical nature of the good or service produced. Each of these will be examined.

Economy of Scale. Economies of scale occur when increased production of a good results in reduced per-unit cost of the output. A great

[18] Aggregation of separate goods to reduce decision-making costs occurs in the private sector as well. For example, restaurants usually offer complete dinners, rather than require the customer to select every item *à la carte.* Tullock, "Federalism," p. 23.

deal of literature deals with economies of scale in the production of public goods and services or of other goods and services often produced by governmental units.[19] However, under many conditions, the economies of scale realized in production are irrelevant to determining the optimum size of a political unit; this is because there is no necessity for the same political unit both to articulate demand for a public good and to produce its supply. Historically, especially in nineteenth-century cities where the fringe areas around the city were relatively uninhabited, it was common for the city to undertake both demand and supply functions for municipal goods and services. More recently, however, with the aggregation of large numbers of people in metropolitan areas, it has become customary for the functions to be separated and the gap bridged by contractual arrangements. The most striking examples of this phenomenon are the Lakewood Plan cities in Los Angeles County, California, where the cities act only as demand coordinators and the city managers as buyers for a consumer cooperative in negotiating with the county, with other cities, special districts, or private producers to purchase all the needed traditional municipal goods and services.[20] Economies of scale that do exist (and empirical studies do not produce much evidence of them for most goods and services for populations in excess of 50,000 to 100,000)[21] can be taken advantage of by a producer who offers the lowest bid for producing the same good or service for more than one demand-articulating unit. Economies of scale then, per se,

[19] Werner Z. Hirsch, "The Supply of Urban Public Services," in Harvey S. Perloff and Lowden Wingo, Jr., eds., *Issues in Urban Economics* (Baltimore: Johns Hopkins Press, 1968).

[20] Robert O. Warren, *Government in Metropolitan Regions: A Reappraisal of Fractionated Political Organization* (Davis, California: Institute of Governmental Affairs, University of California, 1966); *idem,* "A Municipal Services Market Model of Metropolitan Organization," *Journal of the American Institute of Planners,* XXX (August 1964), 193–204.

[21] Few good empirical studies of economies of scale in the production of public goods and services have been made, and results from a majority that have been done cannot be projected to different situations. This is because public goods and services are difficult to analyze. Special problems include the difficulty of measuring outputs and the importance of spatial relationships, such as population densities, unique geographic features (hills, rivers, and bays). Werner Hirsch discusses these problems and summarizes results of empirical studies in "The Supply of Urban Public Services," and "Local versus Area-Wide Urban Government Services," *National Tax Journal,* XVII (December 1964), 331–339.

are not relevant criteria for determining the optimum size of political units to articulate demand, and there is no logical reason why the producing unit need be either public or private, except by historical accident or in some types of protective activity, such as police services.[22]

Boundary Problems. Many public goods are of such a nature that their provision causes boundary problems; that is, the costs or benefits do not accrue completely within the boundary of the political unit providing the public good. For example, when a city provides free parks for its citizens, nonresidents also benefit from their use. If a city maintains a very low level of police protection, negative externalities may accrue to neighboring areas. The existence of spillover problems has often led to the conclusion that political boundaries should be inclusive to the point where all externalities are internalized.[23] This conclusion can be challenged for two reasons.

First, most individuals probably would not want all externalities internalized, as the boundary of the required unit might be extremely wide for some traditionally local functions and, thus, reduce the likelihood of meeting local citizen demands efficiently. For instance, do all highways on the continent need to be planned by the same unit? Even state highways usually link with other states at their boundaries, so it is apparent that cooperation is possible without internalization of all highway planning in a continent-wide hierarchy. What about education? The education a child receives locally may generate positive externalities for the county; then what about the state? The entire nation? The world? There is no more probability of gaining efficiency in handling all externality problems between groups of citizens in different political units by combining all functions in a single unit than there would be in attempting to internalize all externalities in the private sector by putting everyone affected into the same firm.

Second, government units may bargain with one another to

[22] For a discussion related to public utilities, see Harold Demsetz, "Why Regulate Utilities?," *Journal of Law and Economics,* XI (April 1968), 55–65.

[23] For a discussion see Gordon Tullock, "Federalism"; Paul Studenski, *Government of Metropolitan Areas in the United States* (New York: National Municipal League, 1930), pp. 29, 389; Victor Jones, *Metropolitan Government* (Chicago: University of Chicago Press, 1942), ch. III; pp. xix, xxi, 52–84; John C. Bollens, *Special District Governments in the United States* (Berkeley and Los Angeles: University of California Press, 1957), pp. 51–52.

handle positive or negative externalities just as individuals may, and decisions regarding their solution depend on whether internalization in that particular instance is more efficient than some other method. Alternative solutions that are quite common for dealing with intergovernmental externality problems in the United States include functional grants, contracts, and the legislation of minimum standards.[24]

Often, when the activity of a particular political unit (such as a school district) has positive spillovers for a larger area, the political unit representing the citizens in the larger area (such as a state government) will provide functional grants to encourage the local unit to maintain or increase the level of education it provides even though the benefits accrue outside of the small district. National and state objectives are forwarded concurrently with local demands when such grants induce local goverments to expand local governmental goods and services having national or state-wide significance.

Contracting among local government units is a second method of dealing with externalities. For instance, a county may contract with a city to make the city's library facilities available to county residents.

Externality problems may also be dealt with through legislation of minimum standards on a higher political level. For instance, a city may have a low demand for sewage disposal because it simply dumps the sewage into a river and only downstream users feel the damages. A higher political unit, representing a larger constituency, may determine that the costs of sewage disposal should be borne by the city and impose standards that must be met before the effluent can be dumped into the river. The standards would then reduce the negative externality that had been accruing to downstream users.

The boundary problems of externalities can be dealt with within the framework of externalities presented in Chapter 2, the only difference being that, here, the participants may be governmental units representing affected individuals instead of the private parties or unorganized individuals themselves. Even if boundary problems are not the most important consideration, supply conditions are still likely to be important in influencing the area within which provision or production should take place within a single political unit. The problem is that different specific functions require different areas for most efficient provision. For example, air pollution control appears to require "air shed" boundaries for efficient control, for in any lesser area, the effects may be

---

[24] These alternatives are discussed in more detail in following chapters.

negated by polluters locating outside of the political boundaries but still within the air shed. It appears that management of rivers for power production and flood water control is most efficiently performed in a river basin area, although, often, river basin boundaries do not coincide with other political unit boundaries. Effective fire protection, on the other hand, can be provided by a single plant for only a relatively small area because of the importance of travel time from the station house to the source of the fire. Thus, fire districts must be quite small, and larger districts may simply have to be an aggregate of many duplicative small units affording no savings in per unit production costs. Appropriate school district boundaries will vary with the level of education provided. Elementary schools may produce most services within very small neighborhoods. Junior high schools may cover larger areas, high schools still larger ones, with areas still larger for community colleges, state universities, and, finally, national research-oriented universities that draw students on a nationwide basis.

In an extremely large number of economic functions, public demand articulation has proved more efficient than complete reliance on private market demand. These functions have no common boundaries; each must be looked at separately to determine the most efficient area that a producing organization can supply. Even then, it is not necessary for the producing unit to have the same boundaries as the political unit that expresses the demand for the good or service.

Technological supply conditions are usually an important consideration in determining the efficient production of any good and service. A priori, however, one can draw few conclusions concerning optimum producing units in general. Again, every function must be examined in its own right. Empirical studies do indicate, however, that since reduction in costs per unit of production for most municipal goods and services does not continue beyond population sizes of 50,000 to 100,000 people in average-density cities,[25] it is likely that many producers of similar services may continue to function efficiently in metropolitan areas of the United States today.

The Multiplicity of Public Goods. Multiplicity is important on the supply as well as the demand side for public goods. For example, considerable savings may be realized by having the production of several

[25] Hirsch, "The Supply of Urban Public Services"; *idem,* "Local versus Area-wide Government Services."

public goods undertaken by the same producing unit. The same unit that repairs streets in summer may be able to clear snow in winter; the producer of high school education may be an efficient producer of elementary and community college education; the producer and distributor of water may also be an efficient collector and processor of sewage. In many instances, such multiple-production functions may best be performed by the same producer even though the boundaries for the goods and services are not identical. A choice must be made between having hundreds of producers, perhaps requiring very high supervision costs, and having fewer producers who may be able to operate at a lower unit cost while not meeting individual preferences as closely as would be the case if each public good were produced for an area optimum for its own requirements.

It is unlikely that either assigning each activity to a different political unit or assigning all public activities to the same political unit would be the optimal solution. Recent theoretical analysis of public and private hierarchies by Downs and Tullock,[26] and an empirical analysis by Williamson,[27] lend strength to the argument that there are limits to the size of an efficiently functioning hierarchy; but evidence is not yet developed to indicate the most efficient size for any particular production process or to what extent mechanized and electronic data processing will permit an increase in effective sizes in the future.[28]

The Maintenance of Options

Both individuals and leaders of political units have a stake in preventing their subjugation to the monopoly power of any single other individual or organizational unit. To strike better bargains in everyday transactions as well as to provide for unpredictable future events, the individual or single unit must maintain options of recourse. This is accomplished in several ways in relationships between the individual and

---

[26] Anthony Downs, *Inside Bureaucracy* (Boston: Little, Brown, 1967); Gordon Tullock, *The Politics of Bureaucracy* (Washington, D.C.: Public Affairs Press, 1965).

[27] Oliver Williamson, "Hierarchical Control and Optimum Firm Size," *The Journal of Political Economy,* LXXV (April 1967), 123–138.

[28] William Starbuck, "Organization Growth and Development," in James G. March, ed., *Handbook of Organizations* (Chicago: Rand McNally, 1965).

political units as well as between representatives of different political groups.

Essentially, an individual dealing with a political unit has two or three options available to ensure the output he will receive from the public sector. First, he can rely on choosing between alternative delegates or political entrepreneurs for control of a political unit whose provision of a good or service affects him. Second, if one political unit does not satisfy his needs, he can change the arena of action by seeking recourse to another; for instance, steps toward integration were effected through recourse to the Supreme Court rather than to local governmental units in the South, or a corrupt city official may have to be dealt with by county or state law enforcement officers. Very few political units hold a complete monopoly with respect to their services, although in some respects, city governments come close to monopoly with regard to municipal-type services. Third, if an individual is unsatisfied with the action of political units where he resides, he may change his location and opt into a different set of government units. Dissatisfaction with city services, especially education, may have been an important factor in the movement of high-income families to the suburbs where they could join with neighbors who also wanted a higher level of educational services for their children. All three of these options for dealing with public and private problems are important to the individual, and their very existence may elicit more responsiveness from governmental units.

The maintenance of options is also essential for political leaders who must deal with other political units in solving problems and in meeting the demands of their constituencies. A prime example is the functioning of the Lakewood Plan for cities in Los Angeles County, where the city managers encourage alternative producers to enter bids for services traditionally provided by the County. Some of them underbid the County, resulting both in lower costs for the city and, eventually, in the lowering of prices by the County to avoid losing customers.[29]

In the process of maintaining options, political leaders may also try to create monopoly positions for themselves. Their attempts, however, are usually thwarted when individuals exercise their alternatives for solving public and private problems and other political leaders exert themselves to prevent the monopoly from taking shape. In this

[29] A detailed analysis of the Lakewood Plan is included in Chapter 5.

sense, there is true control over each political unit by competing political units that simply cannot be provided by hierarchical organization. This point was emphasized in *The Federalist*:

> In the compound republic of America, the power surrendered by the people is first divided between two distinct governments and then the portion allotted to each subdivided among distinct and separate departments. Hence, a double security arises to the rights of the people. The different governments will control each other, at the same time that each will be controlled by itself.[30]

The independent units do appear to be able to maintain some degree of control over their own organization and, if supported by their constituents, over the activities most important to those constituents. For example, a small city may be able to veto the construction of a through freeway designed primarily to serve citizens outside its boundaries. To the extent that political units maintain veto positions, they are able to prevent the imposition of political externality costs on themselves and their constituents, and such maintenance may lead closer to Pareto-optimal situations. This is because a political unit possessing veto power can force mutually agreeable solutions to problems that affect it and other political units, much as actors in any market-place where voluntary consent is the rule do not enter into transactions without anticipating benefits. The exploration of bargaining and veto points in Mary Parker Follett's *Creative Experience*[31] indicates how the inability of one hierarchy to impose its will on another may lead to bargaining and encourage a search for formerly unrecognized mutually beneficial solutions to problems. The result of the conflict, in that case, is that both parties are better off where, with a solution imposed by a hierarchy, one may have been better off and the other worse off.

The maintenance of options and the ability to prevent the imposition of political externality costs on oneself are both related to the problem of change over time. Changes in individual tastes and in the technology and knowledge available for meeting them will occasion demands for new public goods and perhaps will remove demands for old public goods. The flexibility of a multioption polycentric public sector may be essential for adapting to changing conditions because it

[30] James Madison, Federalist No. 51 in *The Federalist* (New York: Modern Library, n.d.), p. 339.

[31] Follett, *Creative Experience* (London: Longmans, Green, 1930).

more reasonably provides some appropriate political unit (or the opportunity to create a new one) to advocate the change and to compete with established units seeking to retain status quo. The adaptability to change would probably be seriously hindered if the public sector were monopolistically and hierarchically organized, so that the existing interests could not be replaced or overcome as changing conditions require.[32] The problem of change in a technologically advanced society places a high premium on adaptability, a quality probably far more characteristic of a polycentric public economy than of a hierarchical one.

SUMMARY

This chapter began with a conceptual analysis of social interaction costs, defined as costs incurred when individuals cooperate to undertake joint action. These costs include decision-making costs (the actual time, money, and effort of bargaining) and potential political externality costs (costs imposed on any individual when, as part of a group, he is forced to undertake action that does not benefit him). The analysis indicated that the least costly social action for many objectives will be by means of political organization under a decision-making rule of less than voluntary consent.

Alternative techniques for reducing decision-making costs were then discussed, including costs of participation, delegation, and leadership. Finally, an analysis of the important factors related to size and scope of political units was undertaken. In looking at demand articulation within single units, it was concluded that individual demands are most effectively set forth when the individuals are members of small homogeneous units. But it was also observed that, because boundaries differ for use of various public goods, the optimal size of the political unit articulating the demand for the good may also differ.

With respect to supply conditions, it was concluded that economies of scale per se are not important whenever there is a possibility of separat-

---

[32] For a discussion of bureaucracy and responsiveness and innovation, see Victor A. Thompson, *Bureaucracy and Innovation* (University, Ala.: University of Alabama Press, 1969); for examples of problems, see critiques of some major city school systems such as New York City's in Marilyn Gittell and T. Edward Hollander, *Six Urban School Districts* (New York: Praeger, 1968).

ing the producing unit from the political demand-articulating unit. Boundary problems were examined and it was concluded that hierarchical control of externalities is in itself an inadequate goal, since this sole criterion would create excessively large units; also, externalities can be accounted for by means other than internalization in a single hierarchy. An examination of the multiplicity of public goods indicated that some may be efficiently grouped in production by the same unit whereas others may need alternative producers.

The problem of maintaining options and the desirability of flexibility to change were considered in some depth, indicating that these include some of the most telling arguments in support of the polycentric organization of the public sector.

Chapter 4

THE STRUCTURE AND COORDINATION OF
THE STATE AND LOCAL PUBLIC ECONOMY

INTRODUCTION

The previous chapters have dealt with the nature of economic goods and services not adequately provided through voluntary activity and political methods for obtaining them. Both discussions treated the public economy in a conceptual sense only. However, if the preceding theoretical constructs have been based on assumptions that are characteristic of the American public economy, one could predict that the approaches described as efficient in Chapter 3 would illustrate the actual functioning of that economy with fair accuracy. The assumptions included: scarcity of economic resources, methodological individualism, self-interest and individual rationality. These assumptions were combined with assertions based on observation that individuals have diverse tastes for public, as well as private, goods and that public goods and services themselves possess diverse characteristics. Some of the implications suggested in Chapter 3 were: (1) that many different political units covering a variety of areas and using a variety of decision-making rules will emerge to deal efficiently with the diverse public goods and externality problems; and (2) that individuals will attempt to preserve options to escape monopoly control by any single political unit or small set of individuals within that unit.

If empirical examination discloses that these situations do exist and even dominate some specific parts of the American economy, it would indicate that the theoretical structures used here will promote an understanding of the structure and functioning of the American public economy. At the very least, supporting empirical evidence would not rule out the usefulness of the approach. The results may also encourage a continuing detailed examination of specific metropolitan governmental systems and functional problems within the public choice framework.

The empirical descriptions in this chapter follow the conceptual framework developed in previous chapters. First, some features of governmental units functioning in the state and local public economy will be briefly described. More detailed descriptions are readily available elsewhere, but this presentation is sufficient to illustrate the variety of units active in the public economy. Second, coordinating mechanisms will be discussed in relation to the processes for articulating demand, providing supply, and financing public goods and services. The alternative methods —the market system, hierarchical organization, bargaining, voting, and adjudication—will be examined as they operate between citizens and political units and in intragovernmental and intergovernmental relations.

Before analysis of specific features is undertaken in succeeding chapters, the following general descriptions will illustrate the extent to which characteristics of the American public economy conform with those of a theoretically "efficient" public economy. To assist in an evaluation of the predictive usefulness of the theoretical framework, we will also examine the origin and stability of some anomalies.[1]

STRUCTURE OF THE PUBLIC ECONOMY

Several kinds of political units are operative in the state and local public economy. While configurations and relationships among the units differ from state to state, a general classification will serve for this analysis. The most numerous units are the general governments (municipalities and counties) and special purpose districts. The special districts may be either independent or dependent on another governmental unit and may cover subcounty to multistate areas. Many states also establish commissions that function somewhat independently of the state government but have statewide responsibilities.

---

[1] The analysis of anomalies in the public economy is similar to the analysis of irregularities in the private economy associated with the study of industrial organization. For an example, see Richard Caves, *American Industry: Structure, Conduct, Performance* (Englewood Cliffs, N.J.: Prentice-Hall, 1964).

Source of Authority

Political units vary in their independence from other political units. The degree of independence may be analyzed with the aid of two distinctions, although few pure types will be found in empirical cases. The major distinctions are between constitutional and legislative independence and between operative independence and dependence. Constitutional independence exists whenever a political unit is granted specific authority in either a state or national constitution and that authority cannot be altered by the unit itself or by another political unit without recourse to constitutional change. State governments possess powers delegated by both the United States and their own state constitutions. In some states, municipalities are granted constitutional authority to undertake certain activities which the state government cannot alter except by change in the constitution itself.

Legislative independence for a political unit is granted by a general government and may be altered or revoked. While correlation is not perfect, units that possess independent revenue authority are usually identified as operationally independent; those that are subject to detailed supervision by a general government and lack independent revenue authority are termed operationally dependent units. This division, based on revenue authority, places municipalities, counties, and many special districts into the operationally independent category, with some special districts considered as dependent parts of other political units. It is essential to keep in mind the source of authority for political units in examining their role and participation in the public economy.

General Governments

State Governments. State governments are characterized by constitutional independence and a separation of executive, legislative, and judicial powers similar to that of the national government; in many states, the executive branch itself may contain several separately elected officials not subject to the governor's control. State agencies may function with a high degree of constitutional and legislative operational independence (including independent revenue authority), although they are nominally subject to statutory and executive control. In most states, the government cannot be pictured as a neat hierarchical structure, even within the executive branch.

Counties. Counties or parishes are found in all states except Connecticut and Hawaii. Generally, they do not possess independent constitutional authority, but are operated by elected officials who exercise fiscal power under legislative authority of the state; thus, they may be characterized as operationally independent. The degree of legislative control over county activities ranges from those serving virtually as subunits of state government to those possessing home-rule provisions under state constitutional authority.

Municipalities. Often, the state differentiates municipalities by size and allocates authority on that basis. Larger units are usually granted greater discretion. In 1967, roughly 18,000 municipalities in the United States contained 117 million of the nation's 195 million people. The size ranges are extreme; 130 municipalities exceeded populations of 100,000 and contained 43 percent of the population of all municipalities and the smallest 13,000 accounted for only 8 percent of that total.[2]

Townships. The 17,000 existing townships are found in only 21 states, mainly in the rural Northeast and Midwest. While townships exercise varying degrees of authority, they generally serve limited rural needs. Dependent on state legislative authorization, they still may function as operationally independent units with their own elected officials and revenue powers.

Special Districts

School Districts. During 1967, there were 21,782 school districts in the United States. The number has been declining because of rural district consolidation. In 25 states, responsibility for providing education lies completely with the school districts, while the other 25 maintain both independent local school districts and supplemental political units that deal with educational services. With few exceptions, school districts are operationally independent, their citizens electing representatives (usually a school board) and possessing taxing authority, usually limited, or requiring a special levy to exceed certain state-specified levels.

[2] All data on sizes and numbers of governmental units are from U.S. Bureau of the Census, *Census of Governments, 1967* (Washington, D.C.: U.S. Government Printing Office, 1968).

Independent Special Districts. The most varied areas of local government comprise the independent special districts, which are increasing steadily. In 1967, there were 21,000 districts—an increase of about 72 percent from 1952 to 1967. Generally, each special district is created to handle a single specific function. In 1967, the most common stipulated functions included issues concerned with natural resources such as soil conservation, drainage, irrigation and flood control (6,539 units); fire protection (3,665); urban water supply (2,140); housing and renewal (1,565); cemeteries (1,397); sewage disposal (1,233); school buildings (956); highways (774); parks and recreation (613); hospitals (537); and libraries (410). There were also 453 multipurpose special districts.

Most special districts are located within a single county, but some cross not only county lines, but, occasionally, state boundaries as well. To cross a state line, a special district must be approved by the legislature of each state as well as by the national government, the latter because of the U.S. Constitutional clause limiting agreements among independent states.[3]

Students of governmental structure and functioning often regard special districts with disfavor. Indeed, a recent report by the Advisory Commission on Intergovernmental Relations is entitled *The Problem of Special Districts in American Government.*[4] Special districts, in general (and by the ACIR), are usually viewed as inefficient, unresponsive to citizen demands, too small, leading to a fragmented political structure, and obsolete.[5] Ironically, after devoting 70 pages to an analysis of problems of special districts, the ACIR reached the conclusions that

> . . . the creation of special districts is generally the result of the need to: (1) provide an essential service when resort to regular government processes has failed to produce an acceptable means of providing the service through existing units of general local government (i.e., counties, cities, or towns); or (2) otherwise meet a particular local governmental or political problem. . . .

In general, the public appears to be satisfied with services

[3] "No State shall, without the consent of Congress . . . enter into any agreement or compact with another State. . . ." U.S., *Constitution,* Art. I, sec. 10.

[4] Advisory Commission on Intergovernmental Relations, *The Problem of Special Districts in American Government* (Washington, D.C.: U.S. Government Printing Office, 1964).

[5] *Ibid.,* ch. VIII.

received from special districts and, by and large, the districts have resolved the problems which spawned them and have met the demands for public service in an adequate fashion.[6]

In the approach taken in this study, which begins with an analysis of the nature of the public good or service, it will be seen that special districts play an important role in solving problems efficiently. Critiques of special districts will be discussed in Chapter 8, on political reform movements.

Dependent Special Districts. In contrast to operationally independent special districts, dependent special districts are those political units under the direct and formal supervision of another unit of government, usually one of the general governments, that exercise specific functional responsibilities outside the everyday operations of the general government. Dependent special districts range through such areas as air pollution control, airport management and toll bridge authorities. Some of these units may be little more than special taxing areas within the general unit created to provide a higher level of some kind of service to small subareas without financing the improvements from the general treasury. For instance, a county government may designate a small part of the county as a special taxing area for sewage disposal or street lighting. Other dependent special districts will approach independence with some revenue authority. Direct subordination to a general government distinguishes dependent districts and independent special districts, which are subject only to general state (or state and national) legislation.

The variety of local political units in the United States public economy provides a wide range of alternatives for collective action to solve problems and to provide public goods and services. With few exceptions, a citizen is a member of many political units concurrently and, therefore, incurs both opportunities and costs: opportunities to seek solutions to problems by means of an area unit appropriate to the scale of the problem and under appropriate decision-making rules, and the costs of keeping track of the prolific units with which he is blessed. Because this rich environment offers every chance to examine the manner in which individuals seek solutions to collective problems, it deserves considerably more study than it generally has been accorded.

[6] *Ibid.,* p. 74.

COORDINATION IN THE PUBLIC ECONOMY

An analysis of interaction between individuals and political units, among political units, and within political units will add empirical data as to how the diverse political units function in the public economy and how coordination is achieved.

A comprehensive analysis of alternatives for coordinating individual activities is contained in Dahl and Lindblom's *Politics, Economics and Welfare*.[7] Dahl and Lindblom, however, use "social welfare functions" in measuring the achievements of alternative organizing modes. The social welfare function approach has been explicitly rejected throughout this analysis because it assumes away the most difficult problem in allocating scarce resources: identification of individual demand in the construction of the social welfare function. Dahl and Lindblom's discussion of voting, hierarchies, the price system, and bargaining is useful, however, regardless of the social welfare concept.

Individual/Political Unit Relations

Voting is generally considered to be the major, if not the only, way citizens reveal their preferences for public goods and services.[8] This misconception has led analysts to conclude that articulation of demand in the political process must be grossly inefficient relative to articulation under the price system.[9] There are several reasons for the relative inefficiency of its expression by ballot. Even supplementing voting by other communication between citizens and their political units is not likely to achieve the efficiency of a market system. However, because the political process is designed to complement the market process precisely where voluntary exchange relationships are not adequate, the combination of voting and other communication may offer the best attainable world and is worthy of analysis for its role in the allocation of scarce resources.

[7] Robert A. Dahl and Charles E. Lindblom, *Politics, Economics and Welfare* (New York: Harper & Row, 1953).

[8] For example, see Committee for Economic Development, *Modernizing Local Government* (New York: July 1966), Statement by the Research and Policy Committee.

[9] James M. Buchanan, "Individual Choice in Voting and the Market," in *Fiscal Theory and Political Economy* (Chapel Hill: University of North Carolina Press, 1960).

The a priori reasons why voting is not likely to be as efficient as a market exchange have been presented elsewhere, and the brief analysis here focuses on only the major points.[10]

The major differences between voting and market exchange in this connection can be lumped into three broad areas. First is the nature of the alternatives. Voters often face a "blue plate" menu problem, in being forced to allow a single action—a single vote—to express preferences on many issues. The situation does not pose much difficulty when a single issue is being decided (although the system offers the voter only two alternatives rather than offering him a chance to make incremental adjustments among consumption of many goods), but complexities arise when a voter must limit his choice to one of two delegates who will act for him on a great variety of issues, because it is unlikely he will find that his preferences coincide completely with either of the potential delegates. In the market, on the other hand, he would generally be able to choose packageable goods to suit his own preferences. A priori, the choice for delegates will be more efficient if the delegate is responsible for a small related set of public activities rather than for a large number of unrelated public activities because in the more limited area, the individual voter has more chance of finding a delegate whose positions coincide with his own.

A second problem is the degree to which voters are responsible for their choices. In the market, where an individual directly bears the costs and benefits of his actions, he has an incentive to examine the consequences of his actions closely. In voting however, the consequences of his single vote may be quite small or even imperceptible, so he has little incentive to explore the consequences of his action in depth. The relative unimportance of his vote justifies the voter's lack of interest in the analysis of political issues; but the lack of analysis may also lead him to choose poor alternatives in the public sector.

A third reason that voting is likely to be less efficient than market exchange is the equal weight all votes are given, no matter how intense the preferences of the individual voters. An individual who is strongly in favor of an issue is given no more weight in the voting process than

[10] For example, see Buchanan, "Individual Choice"; Anthony Downs, *An Economic Theory of Democracy* (New York: Harper & Row, 1957); Gordon Tullock, "Federalism: Problems of Scale," *Public Choice,* VI (Spring 1969), 23; James M. Buchanan and Gordon Tullock, *The Calculus of Consent* (Ann Arbor: University of Michigan Press, 1962), pp. 125–45.

one who is a relatively indifferent opponent. Both of these individuals could better their positions, from their own points of view, if the individual with intense preferences could barter with the indifferent opponent in exchange for his opponent's voting favorably on the issue. When several issues are involved over time, as in legislative sessions, vote trading and logrolling are likely to provide for increased efficiency of a voting process.[11] Since most individual votes cast within a political unit are secret and of a single type, a market for votes to help differentiate intense and ambivalent feelings among the electorate cannot be established.

The joint product of voting choices, the all-or-none nature of alternatives, the lack of direct responsibility, and the equal weight given diverse preferences are likely, therefore, to make the voting process less efficient than the market for articulating the demands of individuals for public goods and services. It must be remembered, however, that in spite of its weaknesses, the voting process may be superior to any other process for relating demand to the allocation of scarce resources in many contexts.

If voting were the *only* communication among individuals and political delegates, potential delegates, or political leaders, one would have to be pessimistic about the efficiency of collective action among large groups—as are many analysts of voting behavior.[12] However, voting is not the only, and may not even be the most important, means by which citizens reveal their preferences for public goods and services. Some of the other methods include direct communication with delegates, such as letter-writing or direct conversation with a political leader; indirect communication, such as hiring a lobbyist who, in turn, directly communicates with the political leader; public opinion polls; and grassroot expression of demands injected into the political party structure. All of these techniques help mitigate major problems of voting—they

[11] For analyses of the efficiency-improving results of vote trading, see James S. Coleman, "The Possibility of a Social Welfare Function," *American Economic Review*, LVI (December 1966), 1105–1122; Buchanan and Tullock, *Calculus of Consent*, pp. 131–45.

[12] See, for example, Angus Campbell et al., *The American Voter* (New York: Wiley, 1960), pp. 541–48; Bernard R. Berelson, et al., *Voting* (Chicago: University of Chicago Press, 1954), pp. 309–311. For an alternative view, see V. O. Key, Jr., *The Responsible Electorate* (Cambridge, Mass.: Harvard University Press, 1966), pp. 150–51; V. O. Key, Jr., *Public Opinion and American Democracy* (New York: Knopf, 1961), pp. 556–58.

permit the expression of opinion on individual issues and permit those
with either high or low urgency of demands to express them more or
less intensely rather than with an equal-weighted vote. The ultimate
check of the voting itself induces the political delegate or potential delegate to pay attention to all the information he can obtain on citizen
preferences if he wishes to be elected or retain office.

Individual citizens will also use direct communication techniques to
deal directly with employees in government bureaucracies, and employees generally recognize some need to be responsive, to avoid any indication of unsatisfactory relationships with clients that would reflect on
the employees' superiors and eventually on the political leaders. In addition to individuals' recourse to voting and direct confrontation with a
single political unit, there are many political units with overlapping
jurisdictions in the United States; if an individual is not satisfied with
the services of a particular unit, he may take his demands to another,
and often competing, unit. In general, individuals will attempt to influence the output of public goods and services whenever the benefits
they anticipate from such efforts exceed their costs, and this will lead to
the use of a variety of techniques, depending on the strength of the
interests involved.

Relations between individuals and political units exist on the supply
as well as on the demand side. The means of allocating resources for
production of public goods are similar to the means employed by private
producers. Factors of production, including labor, material inputs, and
capital equipment, are usually purchased in private markets in competition with other potential users of the factors.[13] Organization on the
supply side will consist of a mixture of relatively pure market relationships, bargaining (especially where the political unit is the only purchaser for some factor or kind of labor and the factors or workers are
few in number or are organized), and hierarchical relationships, the
latter existing primarily within the producing unit itself.

Political units possess one power that other units functioning in the
market do not—that of eminent domain, whereby a piece of property
can be condemned and for "fair" compensation acquired for some
public purpose. The logic of using eminent domain powers to avoid
high-cost bargaining by individuals whose property is strategic to a
specific public undertaking is clear enough, but the net results of such
actions are not. This particular issue is too complex to treat within this

[13] The military draft is a substantial exception.

monograph, but interested readers are referred to Frank Michelman's excellent discussion of the issue in "Property, Utility, and Fairness: Comments on the Ethical Foundations of 'Just Compensation' Law." [14] His conclusions are that the present division between compensable and noncompensable harm from public activity diverges from what would be considered "fair" in an economic analysis framework, but that it is about as perfect as court decisions can achieve.

One other relationship between individuals and political units is extremely important—that of the individual as a compulsory taxpayer to the unit. Given the positive costs of obtaining voluntary agreement among large groups, compulsory taxation is a necessary response to the free-rider problem for the provision of public goods and services. Taxes, however, may or may not reflect benefits received for which the taxes are allegedly paid. Even if the taxpayer has received the benefits, he would profit by a reduction in taxes because his reduction in payment would not noticeably affect the total provision of government services.

Individuals can logically have conflicting attitudes toward taxes: first, to be equitable, taxes should really reflect the benefits I receive as closely as possible; second, it is always okay for others to be taxed to pay for my benefits. The closer the tax paid relates to the service received, the more efficient the public economy is likely to be. The very fact that individuals demonstrate that they have an effective demand for a public good or service by paying for it assures that they value that production more than alternative uses of resources. To the extent that noneffective demands are met (those characterized by "I want and need it, but only if someone else pays for it"), the value of the resources being used for consumption is greater than the benefits that individual consumers perceive in using up the resources.

The treatment of all taxation in a benefits-received framework, rather than relating some taxes to ability to pay, does not eliminate consideration of income redistribution or policies to achieve economic stability, but treats them as desired states of affairs for which there must be an effective demand if they are to be achieved. [15] The payment of taxes for

---

[14] *Harvard Law Review*, LXXX (April 1967), 1165–1258.

[15] The division between benefits-received and ability-to-pay taxation is common, as is separation of resource allocative, redistributive, and stabilizing activity. Richard A. Musgrave, *The Theory of Public Finance* (New York: McGraw-Hill, 1959), chs. 1, 4 and 5.

Relating all three functions to individual demands places all taxation

which no benefits are received may be characterized as a political externality cost, and individuals who feel that, over time, the political externality costs exceed their net benefits from participation in the political unit have the option of attempting to change the constitutional decision-making rules or of moving to another political unit. Where mobility is impossible, such individuals may have an incentive to refuse to comply with other rules of the political unit and may resort to "revolt" or revolution to obtain the changes they feel are necessary to bring them long-run net benefits from political unit membership. The possibility of revolution or migration does provide limited options for individuals who are dissatisfied with the political situation, and that threat plus a demand for "equity" on the part of a large number of citizens may provide incentive to develop relatively equitable political structures.

Intraorganizational Coordination

The techniques employed to coordinate intraorganization political units are apparently similar to those used by any other organization—some combination of hierarchical ordering and bargaining. Two problems may increase problems of political unit management vis-a-vis management of a private firm. They are the difficulty of measuring the output of many public goods and services and the opportunity for formally subordinate agencies or individuals to form alliances with clients to strengthen their bargaining power relative to officially superior individuals. Theoretical analyses of public organizations within the framework used in this analysis are presented in Gordon Tullock's *The Politics of Bureaucracy*[16] and in Anthony Downs' *Inside Bureaucracy*.[17] Attempts are being made to introduce program budgeting and cost-benefit analysis to strengthen hierarchical management but, these techniques are still insufficiently developed for many public activities.[18]

---

on a benefits-received basis without ruling out income redistribution and stabilizing activity. Income redistribution is analyzed within this framework in Chapter 7.

[16] Tullock, *The Politics of Bureaucracy* (Washington, D.C.: Public Affairs Press, 1965).

[17] Downs, *Inside Bureaucracy* (Boston: Little, Brown, 1967).

[18] For a good collection of readings, see Joint Economic Committee, *The Analysis and Evaluation of Public Expenditures: The PPB System,* 3 vols. (Washington, D.C.: U.S. Government Printing Office, 1969).

Since these issues are examined elsewhere and are not essential to this study, further analysis is unnecessary here.

Intergovernmental Coordination

Intergovernmental coordination occurs between units of approximately equal powers, that is, between cities, between cities and counties and independent special districts, and between units at different levels, such as federal-state or state-local. Most intergovernmental coordination takes place under either hierarchical or bargained agreements. Federal regulation of state and local governments by restrictive legislation, such as the imposition of minimum standards of performance for some good or service, is an example of hierarchical coordination. Even more common is the assignment of certain responsibilities by state governments to local units. Hierarchical coordination may also be achieved through the use of tax incentives, as in a case where a state provides a tax credit to individuals who pay stipulated amounts for local government services. The essential feature of hierarchical coordination is that it is initiated by a governmental unit authorized to act in a manner to influence the action of other political units. The actions of the higher unit may be either coercive (as in restrictive legislation), or simply provide opportunities to influence local government action (as in providing tax credits).

Examples of bargained intergovernmental cooperation are much more numerous, although most analyses have dealt with hierarchical, rather than bargained, relationships. Since bargained agreements rest on the consent of both parties, they offer an opportunity for intergovernmental cooperation where both units feel that they will benefit from the arrangement. Bargained agreements exist between political units of the same and of different levels.

The major agreements among different governmental levels comprise the functional grant programs.[19] In general, these are programs where a higher-level government, federal or state, agrees to pay a lower-

[19] For most state and federal grant programs, the term "grant" is misleading because the programs are not "gifts" to governmental units, but quid pro quo contracts requiring the receiving governmental unit to undertake certain activities in exchange for payment by the grantor.

For examples, see Advisory Commission on Intergovernmental Relations, *The Role of Equalization in Federal Grants* (Washington, D.C.: U.S. Government Printing Office, 1964); Office of Economic Opportunity, *Catalog of Federal Programs for Individual and Community Improvement* (Washington, D.C.: U.S. Government Printing Office, 1965). For analyses, see Morton

level governmental unit a certain amount for undertaking a particular productive action (the federal government has over 400 programs). Grants are often employed where anticipated benefits from local government action will spill over beyond the local boundaries. The higher government unit then acts as a representative of individuals who will benefit from the spillovers by effectively demanding increases in output of the good. Such is the common practice to increase local unit provision of education, public health services, some police services, and most welfare-type services—functions where the benefits are difficult to measure and some nationwide minimum standard appears desirable. There is no question that functional grant programs, when viewed as a whole, are extremely complex, but individuals involved in the functional fields appear to understand the grant requirements and to make use of them in ways mutually beneficial to the grantee and grantor.

Two types of intergovernmental cooperation are especially common between political units of a similar level. These are cooperative production and contracting to buy or sell entire packages of public goods outputs.[20] Under cooperative production, two or more governmental units act together to produce a public good or service for the citizens of their units. Contracted production occurs when one political unit simply pays a public or private producing unit to provide a public good or service for its citizens. The extreme examples of contracting are found in the Lakewood Plan cities (named after the City of Lakewood—the first complete contract city) of Los Angeles, California, where the cities function essentially as consumer cooperatives, purchasing an entire range of municipal goods and services from the county, other cities, and private

---

Grodzins, *The American System* (Chicago: Rand McNally, 1966), pp. 60–153; Selma J. Mushkin and John F. Cotton, *Sharing Federal Funds for State and Local Needs* (New York: Praeger, 1969).

[20] For examples and analyses, see Oregon University, Bureau of Municipal Research and Service, "Local Intergovernmental Cooperation in the Tri-County Area," Information Bulletin No. 150 (November 1966); Council of State Governments, *Patterns of Intergovernmental Cooperation* (Chicago: Council of State Governments, 1959); W. Brooke Graves, *American Intergovernmental Relations* (New York: Scribner, 1964); Robert O. Warren, "A Municipal Services Market Model of Metropolitan Organization," *Journal of the American Institute of Planners* (August 1964), pp. 193–203; Advisory Commission on Intergovernmental Relations, *A Handbook for Interlocal Agreements and Contracts* (Washington, D.C.: U.S. Government Printing Office, 1967).

vendors.[21] Cooperative, and especially contracted, provision of public goods and services facilitates the achievement of several goals simultaneously. First, the demand articulating unit can be relatively small and homogeneous; second, the producing unit can be of whatever size is most efficient for production of the good or service; and third, the city manager of the demand articulating unit operates as a knowledgeable purchaser in dealing with alternative producers to get the best price for his clients, the citizens. Intergovernmental contracting among cities, counties, special districts, and private producers is a rapidly growing area of intergovernmental cooperation and promises to become increasingly prevalent in the future.

Councils of Government, commonly known as COGs, are a special coordinating device falling somewhere between a special district and a cooperative activity.[22] The Councils, composed of representatives of counties and major cities (and sometimes of minor cities and special districts as well), serve as a forum in which common problems can be discussed. There were ten COGs in 1966, and their successes are mixed. Their decision-making rule tends to be one of unanimity. They have no formal authority over their members, but provide not only a forum, but an arena in which bargaining and negotiation can take place to find mutually agreeable solutions to common problems. COGs are likely to gain importance as problems are dealt with on an area-wide basis, but as yet, they have not passed beyond the high decision-making costs (but low political externality costs) due to their use of voluntary consent as a prerequisite to action.

SUMMARY AND CONCLUSIONS

The brief and general description of the variety of governmental units and the different methods by which interaction occurs between individuals and political units and among political units serves to indicate that the public economy is extremely complex. At least two interpretations of this complexity are possible. The first does not refute the hy-

[21] Robert O. Warren, *Government in Metropolitan Regions* (Davis, Calif.: Institute of Governmental Affairs, University of California Press, 1966).

[22] Advisory Commission on Intergovernmental Relations, *Metropolitan Councils of Government* (Washington, D.C.: U.S. Government Printing Office, 1966).

pothesis that the varieties of political units and coordinating mechanisms
are necessary and efficient in dealing with the variety of public goods
and services and diverse preferences of individuals. The second interpretation is that such a complex system simply cannot be efficient and work-
able. Both conclusions have been drawn by analysts of metropolitan
governmental systems. The following three chapters will present analyses
of governmental systems (Los Angeles County and Dade County,
Florida), specific functional problem areas (education and air pollution),
and income redistribution. The purpose of this examination is to
determine whether the political structure and functioning that has
evolved is an efficient response to the problems faced. Following these
analyses will be a discussion of proposed recommendations for governmental change in metropolitan areas based on the view that the present
public economy is simply chaotic. The value of traditional approaches
to the study of the public economy will then be compared with the approach used in this study. The analysis of political reform movements in
Chapter 8 will help clarify the differences in assumptions and conclusions
in the two approaches.

Chapter 5

METROPOLITAN AREA SYSTEMS OF GOVERNMENT: LOS ANGELES AND DADE COUNTIES

INTRODUCTION

A general description of the structure and coordination of the state and local public economy demonstrates that it is extremely complex. An examination of two metropolitan area systems of government—Los Angeles County, California and Dade County, Florida—will help to determine if this complexity is a systematic response to the different demands of individuals for diverse public goods and services.

Los Angeles and Dade County areas were selected for comparative analysis for several reasons. Both are rapidly growing urban areas, both have large populations requiring urban-type services in unincorporated areas, and both have undergone significant changes in their governmental structures since World War II. They also offer an instructive contrast in evolving structures of government: Los Angeles has become increasingly complex in numbers of units and relationships among units, while Dade County has been undergoing one of very few metropolitan reform experiments.[1] Finally, since both systems have been analyzed elsewhere, information is readily available.

[1] "Metropolitan government reform," and "political reform movements" refer to the tradition of writing on metropolitan area governments based on ideas crystallized in the 1920s and repeated as solutions to urban area governmental problems in the 1960s.

Generally, the recommendations include area-wide metropolitan government, area-wide equalization of services, and at-large, often nonpartisan, elections. Some political reform recommendations are analyzed in Chapter

In the following discussion, a few of the previous analyses will be relied upon heavily. This procedure has both advantages and disadvantages. A major advantage is, of course, that these comprehensive sources provide examples for this study that would otherwise have required extensive empirical work. The disadvantage is that the analysts of the systems may not have provided information relevant for comparisons based on economic approaches. Fortunately, Robert O. Warren's study of Los Angeles County, *Government in Metropolitan Regions: A Reappraisal of Fractionated Political Organization*,[2] is adaptable to the public choice approach because it attempts to identify the rationality of the structure to meet individual demands. Despite some similarity between Warren's approach and that of this monograph, however, the former does not provide empirical data on costs and benefits of government production to support an efficiency analysis. This, however, is a general problem in analysis of public goods and services and is not unique to Warren's study.

Edward Sofen's *Miami Metropolitan Experiment*[3] and Reinhold Wolff's *Miami Metro*[4] were primary sources for the examination of Dade County. Their approach is considerably different from mine; they base normative conclusions on political reform assertions that are completely unsupported by any explicit theoretical structure or empirical analysis. Like others, these analyses lack data on the costs and benefits of government provision and production of public goods and services. While my conclusions might differ from those drawn by Sofen and Wolff, much of their analysis is useful for exploring questions raised by the theoretical constructions in this study.

Discussion of the two metropolitan systems is designed not to determine which is more efficient (data are simply not available for such a comparison), but to demonstrate the usefulness of theoretical concepts gleaned from economics in gaining an understanding of the functioning

---

8 of this study. A history of the literature is contained in Robert O. Warren, *Government in Metropolitan Regions: A Reappraisal of Fractionated Political Organization* (Davis, Calif.: Institute of Governmental Affairs, University of California Press, 1966), ch. 1–3.

   [2] *Ibid.*

   [3] Sofen, *Miami Metropolitan Experiment* (Bloomington: Indiana University Press, 1963).

   [4] Wolff, *Miami Metro* (Coral Gables, Fla.: University of Miami, Bureau of Business and Economic Research, 1960).

of specific complex metropolitan public economies. While this is not the only explanation possible, it suggests the value of further analysis along these lines and provides a framework for further empirical work, from which hard conclusions on the relative efficiency of alternative organizations for metropolitan area government may be drawn.

THE LOS ANGELES AREA

With a 1969 population of 7.0 million, Los Angeles County is the second largest standard metropolitan statistical area in the United States.[5] Its 4,060 square miles spread over an area four times as large as Rhode Island and nearly as large as Connecticut. Los Angeles County contains 233 local government units, all but 8 of which have property-taxing power.[6] Of these units, 76 are municipalities and 16 have populations over 50,000; 40 have populations between 10,000 and 49,999; 8 between 5000 and 9999; and 12 have populations under 5000. There are 95 school districts, 29 water districts, 9 natural resource districts (irrigation and soil conservation), 5 cemetery districts, 4 health districts, 4 park districts, 2 hospital districts, 2 housing and urban renewal districts, 2 library districts, 1 sewer district, 1 transit district, and 3 multipurpose districts dealing with natural resource and water supply. Fifty-six of the districts are not coterminous with other boundaries. In addition to the independent taxing districts, 239 subordinate special taxing areas are managed by the county government. Have these manifold units been created to meet citizen demands and, if so, have they succeeded?

The City of Los Angeles

With 2.9 million people and 455 square miles, the City of Los Angeles is the largest and oldest in Los Angeles County and achieved its present size through both population growth and an extensive annexation and consolidation program.

[5] Population data from: State Controller, *Annual Report of Financial Transactions, 1968–69* (Sacramento, Calif.: State Controller's Office, 1969).

[6] Figures on governmental units are from U.S. Bureau of the Census, *Census of Governments, 1967,* Vol. 1, "Governmental Organization" (Washington, D.C.: U.S. Government Printing Office, 1968), Table 19, pp. 132–133; and Table 22, p. 289.

Prior to 1910, citizens in the rapidly growing area could obtain urban-type services only as members of some municipality. They could move to Los Angeles city or another incorporated area; they could have their area annexed to an existing city; or they could incorporate. (Satisfaction of demands for municipal services appears to have been the major incentive for incorporation.) Many of the new cities, however, lacked an adequate source of water, as the City of Los Angeles held prior Pueblo water rights under Spanish water law and exercised a monopoly over the waters of the Los Angeles River.[7] Under its appropriative rights, the city could not sell water to nearby municipalities, and its monopoly not only served to concentrate growth in the city proper, but led several other municipalities (such as Hollywood) to consolidate with Los Angeles to obtain water supplies.

Eventually, the supply of water from the Los Angeles River became inadequate for the expanding city, and in 1913, Los Angeles brought water to the area from the Owens River, 250 miles' distance. The city was free to sell surplus Owens River water to adjacent areas; instead, it used its monopoly position to engage in an ambitious annexation program. The campaign was so aggressive that an antiannexation league was formed in 1917, and many municipalities incorporated in self-defense. Water shortages still plagued the area, however, and by 1927, Los Angeles had used its water monopoly to induce Sawtell, Eagle Rock, Hyde Park, and Watts to consolidate and had acquired 441 of its present 455 square miles. Los Angeles city policy also precluded maintenance of separate political entities, such as boroughs, within the city for annexed or consolidated areas.[8]

By 1927, Los Angeles had committed its existing water supplies, and its policy shifted. It was no longer feasible to annex areas that were short of water. However, economic growth in Los Angeles and the surrounding area continued, and by the middle 1920s, the city had already considered importing water from the Colorado River. Such a project required approval by Federal authorities and the State legislature, and because of Los Angeles' past monopolistic use of its water supply to encourage annexation, surrounding communities were wary. Thus, to provide water for its own continued growth, Los Angeles was forced

[7] For an analysis of Los Angeles' water monopoly and use to encourage annexation, see Vincent Ostrom, *Water and Politics* (Los Angeles: Haynes Foundation, 1953).

[8] Warren, *Government in Metropolitan Regions*, pp. 63–65.

to enter into a cooperative agreement with several counties and other municipalities and form the Metropolitan Water District.[9] The MWD, which did eventually bring Colorado River water to Southern California, serves only as a wholesaler. Distribution is handled by counties, special districts, and municipalities. The creation of the MWD ended Los Angeles' monopoly of the water supply and the threat of involuntary absorption to fringe-area cities.

At the same time Los Angeles was expanding by using its water monopoly to encourage annexation, it was undertaking contracted arrangements with other municipalities for sewage disposal. It was impossible for Los Angeles to obtain a monopoly in this service, but economies of scale enabled the city to offer its services at a cost lower than the smaller cities'. Beginning in 1905, Los Angeles became a wholesaler for sewage disposal, and by 1930, it was serving some fifteen cities and special districts.[10] In addition to contracting sewage disposal services, Los Angeles now provides several services—primarily, utilities to nearby municipalities and special districts.

Los Angeles County

In 1911, a constitutional amendment permitted counties to adopt home rule charters enabling them to organize and provide municipal-type services formerly undertaken only by cities.[11] Los Angeles County adopted a charter in 1912.[12] Small municipalities and unincorporated areas turned increasingly to the county for efficient production of municipal services as an alternative to annexation to Los Angeles, and by 1930 the county was providing tax collection and assessment, library, and public health services through voluntary agreements with municipalities and special districts.

The development of library services provides an interesting example of the use of available multiple options to efficiently meet citizen demands.[13] In 1913, the county took advantage of the County Free Library Act to establish a system to service unincorporated areas and municipalities that lacked a public library. Areas wanting library service now

[9] *Ibid.*, pp. 75–79; and Ostrom, *Water and Politics,* p. 136.
[10] Warren, *Government in Metropolitan Regions,* p. 82.
[11] *California Constitution,* Article XI, sec. 7½.
[12] Warren, *Government in Metropolitan Regions,* p. 93.
[13] *Ibid.*, pp. 94–97.

had several options, including use of municipal libraries, organizing or joining a special library district, contracting with another jurisdiction, or becoming part of the new county system. By 1950, the county was able to reach a regional scale of operation, serving twenty-one cities with a population totaling 431,221 and unincorporated areas with a population of 941,167. From the time of its formation, the county library service was retained by all but one city incorporating in the county, but during this time, nine cities chose to withdraw from the county, either to adjust to a different service level to meet individual community demands or to obtain a more favorable cost-service ratio.

The county library policy was to provide a uniform level of service throughout the area served, financed by a uniform, earmarked, property tax levy. This uniform level of service and taxation was not as satisfactory to some municipalities as were competitive options. For example, two municipalities, Signal Hill and Vernon, incorporated to protect wealthy industrial tax bases from neighboring cities, found themselves paying high taxes to provide library services to very small populations. Their response was to withdraw from the county system and establish their own municipal libraries; a lower level of library service was provided but tax levies were considerably reduced. If the citizens had demanded equal or higher-level library services, the municipality could still have provided them at tax rates lower than for membership in the county system.

Another group of municipalities to withdraw from the county library system was composed of citizens who had much higher demands for library services. Beverly Hills and San Marino withdrew and provided a higher level of service with higher budget allocations than either the county service or independent library districts of comparable size in the county. It is not clear whether the move resulted in increased tax rates because they had higher-than-average property valuations, and library services at a higher level than the county offered could have been provided without raising tax rates.

In addition to the demand by some municipalities for a higher or lower level of library services than those uniformly provided by the county, others that were satisfied with the level of service per se were not satisfied with its cost because their assessed valuations were higher than average. Burbank, for example, withdrew from the county system and immediately contracted with the same system for identical services at lower cost than the former uniform tax levy.

The alternatives available to citizens for obtaining library services in Los Angeles County have permitted communities to adjust service levels to meet their own preferences at the least cost. Such flexibility and adjustment is an excellent example of the capability of the public economy to provide a public good (the availability of a library) in an efficient manner.

The development of a county library system to provide services at a uniform tax rate, or by contract at a rate equal to cost of services provided, is but one area in which the county has undertaken to provide municipal-type services to both municipalities and unincorporated areas. Other areas of production include public health services, sanitation services, fire protection, county planning and urban zoning, and police protection, all of which have depended on voluntary cooperation between the county, municipalities and special districts. Legislation has prescribed minimum standards in some areas, such as public health, but subareas are free to meet those standards in the most efficient manner. In areas where countywide organization has offered significant economies, the county has tended to become the dominant producer. Where efficient production has been attainable in much smaller units, special districts and municipalities have emerged as the producing agent. By the 1950s, the county was a major producer of municipal services to incorporated and unincorporated areas through a variety of methods; with the incorporation of Lakewood Plan cities, beginning in 1954, efforts culminated in a program whereby, through contracted relationships, a relatively small unit could purchase any public good or service from a larger production unit.[14]

Recent Developments and the Lakewood Plan

Incorporated areas of the county often accused the county of subsidizing unincorporated areas by use of the countywide portion of property taxes to produce for unincorporated areas municipal goods and services paid for in incorporated areas with city taxes. There is considerable question about the extent to which this occurred relative to the extent to which the independent special districts and county taxing districts actually provided sufficient revenue for their own municipal-type services. The contention, however, led existing municipalities to seek annexation or incorporation of unincorporated areas. The county,

[14] *Ibid.*, Chapters VIII and IX, pp. 162–202.

on the other hand (especially department heads of producing organizations), discouraged incorporation or annexation because it might reduce the size and activity of the county production organizations.

The conflict over tax subsidization to unincorporated areas and a desire by existing municipalities to expand their boundaries led to an attempt by Long Beach to annex an unincorporated area called Lakewood in the early 1950s.

Begun by the Lakewood Park Corporation in 1950, Lakewood was a single development with a relatively homogeneous upper-middle-income population of 77,000 in 1953. While Long Beach itself remained officially neutral, annexation proponents advanced a concerted argument that the Lakewood area would never be able to achieve adequate public services under the county and that even if it incorporated, public service levels would still be inadequate because of the area's lack of an industrial tax base. Lakewood residents, on the other hand, appeared satisfied with the level of services provided by the county and did not want either to become part of Long Beach or to incorporate as a separate entity. In the light of continued attempts by Long Beach to annex parts of Lakewood, citizens of the area who wanted to retain autonomous control, rather than to become only a small part of Long Beach, began discussions of a defensive incorporation, but with serious hesitation about creating a municipal structure to produce goods and services commonly provided by city governments. The outcome of these discussions was the creation of the first complete "contract city" in the United States.

Lakewood was incorporated April 16, 1954. The city was organized without any municipal departments, and by the end of the year, it had only ten full-time employees, including a city attorney, city clerk, city administrator, executive secretary to the council, and secretaries. All services were provided through preexisting special districts or by contract with the following county agencies:[15]

County-administered special districts:
 County library district
 Consolidated fire district
 Lakewood sewer maintenance district
 County lighting districts (2)
 County lighting maintenance districts (2)

[15] *Ibid.,* pp. 156–157.

Self-governing special districts:
    County sanitation district No. 3
    Lakewood Park, recreation, and parkway district
    Southeast mosquito abatement district
    School district
County contracts:
    Animal regulation
    Assessment and collection of taxes
    Building inspection services
    Health services
    Emergency ambulance service
    Engineering staff service
    Industrial waste regulation
    Jail facilities
    Law enforcement
    Prosecution of city ordinance violations
    Planning and zoning staff services
    Street maintenance and construction
    Street sweeping
    Treasury and auditor services
    Tree trimming

Several immediate effects followed Lakewood's incorporation, the most important of which included a *reduction* in property tax rates to residents of Lakewood and a shift in county policy toward encouraging the incorporation of contract cities. The reduction in property tax rates was the result of Lakewood's newly acquired eligibility for a share of state-collected automobile excise tax revenue and of grants from the state that are not available to unincorporated areas and formerly had gone directly to the county. The net tax reduction in 1954–55 was $0.25 per $100 of assessed valuation from a total property tax payment for all services (except education) of $1.59 per $100 assessed value.

An additional incentive to incorporation was the Bradley-Burns sales tax law passed by the State legislature in 1956, which permitted counties to levy a countywide sales tax of 1 percent whereas, formerly, only cities had been eligible to levy such taxes. While allegedly voluntary, the law is written in such a way as to encourage both cities and the county to levy the tax, with revenue in incorporated areas going to the municipality and in unincorporated areas to the county. The availability of the new tax offered the promise that incorporated communities might use the revenues to pay for services contracted with the county—thus, either completely avoiding, or at least reducing, the need for imposing a municipal property tax.

The revenue incentive available to incorporated areas, the encouragement of the county for incorporation as a contract city rather than annexation to a producing city, and the desire of many communities to maintain a high level of local control resulted in incorporation of twenty-five new cities between 1954 and 1961. The incorporation of many small and relatively homogeneous communities or specialized land-use areas was possible and efficient because there was no need for each new municipality to be of sufficient size to produce its own municipal services efficiently. Instead, acting as a political demand articulator for the community, it could purchase municipal goods and services at service levels selected by the community from the county or through other governmental arrangements. The population ranges in Lakewood Plan cities in 1960 was from 618 in Bradbury to 88,807 in Downey. Eight cities had populations of less than 5000, and the median was about 14,000. Some of the new municipalities were extremely specialized limited-goal cities that could realize special advantages by avoiding annexation by other jurisdictions, because their preferences for municipal goods and services were quite different from those of neighboring areas and they wanted to meet these demands as efficiently as possible without bearing the costs of the provision of municipal goods and services for others and without receiving levels of public goods and services that they did not desire. Some examples of these communities are presented below.

Rolling Hills. Incorporated in 1957, this area is composed almost exclusively of one- to five-acre estates on the Palos Verdes Peninsula. To cite a representative of Rolling Hills at a legislative hearing: "The city is entirely residential; it is a single-purpose city; there is no industry, no manufacturing. . . . They [the citizens] want to keep it, and they are willing to pay for it." [16]

Dairy Valley. Under threat of annexation and extension of resi-

---

[16] Assembly Interim Committee on Municipal and County Government, "Incorporations," Transcript of Proceedings, Los Angeles, II (July 22, 1958), p. 143.

dential areas into a region containing 580 dairies and 98,586 cows on 12,000 acres of land representing an investment of more than $90,000,000, the City of Dairy Valley was incorporated in 1956. The boundaries of the city are virtually identical to an area zoned for heavy agriculture, with a five-acre minimum to provide protection and encouragement to dairies and to preclude subdivision activity by the county. It was expected that if nearby Artesia had been able to annex the area, the majority in that municipality would have favored a zoning change for residential expansion and would have sought to benefit from the increased tax base of dairy farms while not wanting to expand municipal-type services to the agricultural area. Incorporation was the only sure way for the farmers to protect their own interests, and they did.

Industry. The boundaries of the City of Industry were drawn to include commercial and industrial land. It records a per capita property value of $54,868 for its 638 inhabitants (150 of whom are residents of a sanitarium). Industry was quite satisfied with county-level services, and since its incorporation, has found it unnecessary to levy a municipal property tax because sales tax revenue and other state funds have been sufficient to meet county contract payments. Some property taxes are levied for special districts.

Rolling Hills, Dairy Valley, and Industry are diverse examples of the special-purpose cities incorporated as Lakewood Plan cities since 1954. They are designed to provide public goods and services efficiently by articulating demands as small homogeneous units and purchasing goods and services from efficient producing organizations. Their incorporation served to prevent the imposition of political externalities by neighboring municipalities that wanted to acquire their relatively high tax bases for financing of public goods and services for their own citizens.

Not all consequences of the establishment of Lakewood Plan cities (for either the county or the cities involved) were anticipated by the citizens. Some of the unanticipated consequences, however, appear to be predictable as elements of an efficiently functioning public sector resembling the model discussed in Chapter 3.[17]

The major change in governmental organization was the separation

[17] See discussion in Warren, *Government in Metropolitan Regions,* pp. 224–247; and *idem,* "A Municipal Services Market Model of Metropolitan Organization," *Journal of the American Institute of Planners,* XXX (August 1964), 193–204.

of the unit for articulating demand from the unit producing the good or service. Most political scientists simply do not consider this possibility in examining municipal organization and often draw conclusions for efficient organization based on a production-oriented criterion such as economies of scale. As pointed out, a priori, there is no reason to expect the unit that efficiently articulates demand (a small, relatively homogeneous one) is of a size that will permit production at relatively low costs. This separation of demand and supply considerations also put the city administrator or city manager in a new position. He was no longer concerned with administering production bureaucracies efficiently; instead, he could concentrate on representing consumer interests in negotiating prices and service levels with the producing unit. Citizen-consumer interests, then, were represented by a skilled administrator who functioned as a buyer for a consumer cooperative, rather than as a production-oriented entrepreneur.

In the Lakewood Plan cities, the city administrators immediately became concerned for their bargaining base in dealing with county producing units. The county was not a complete monopolist, in that cities did have the legal authority to undertake their own production of municipal goods and services; but the costs of undertaking such production would have been quite high for the smaller cities. However, the county was relatively limited in the cost range within which it could bargain, being required by law and enforced by grand jury supervision to avoid discriminatory pricing[18] and to use full-cost pricing to avoid subsidizing contract cities from revenues collected in unincorporated areas. Thus, to keep the bigger contract cities as customers, the county had to keep its costs down to those achievable by the cities themselves. Since some of the contract cities were large enough to undertake their own production efficiently if the county did not maintain an efficient and responsive organization, a competitive element entered.

In addition to the constraint on county productive efficiency exercised by the bargaining power of the larger contract cities, city administrators encouraged other potential sellers of municipal services to submit bids in competition with the county. Both private vendors (especially of street sweeping and garbage removal) and other governmental units,

[18] Price discrimination is charging different buyers different prices unrelated to costs. If price discrimination were permitted, the county could charge cities without low-cost alternatives higher prices than it charged cities with low-cost alternatives for the same service.

such as neighboring cities and special districts, had the legal authority to sell to contract cities and could bid against the county for provision of municipal services. In areas where competitive bidding developed, the county was further limited in its exercise of monopolistic power, and cities were able to obtain even more efficient and responsive service. For example, the county decentralized road maintenance and police protection services in response to requests by contract cities, and even went so far as to require county policemen to reside in the city where they were assigned so that police services would be more responsive to individualized city needs.

The county has not always proved efficient and responsive enough, however, and, on occasion, has been underbid by other cities (library services for Irwindale) or by private vendors (street sweeping for several cities), and in some cases, cities have undertaken their own production (especially street sweeping) at lower costs than the prices offered by the county.

The emphasis on consumer satisfaction and comparison of production prices of alternative ways of supplying public goods and services to contract cities also provided an unanticipated benefit in making the producing bureaucracies more efficient internally. Justification of costs to their purchasers involved detailed study of operations and the development of measurements of production units for public goods and services. Governmental producing units, previously exempt from the competitive market pressures common to private firms, had seldom undertaken such searching self-examination.

Summary and Conclusions on Los Angeles Area Governments

The present structure and functioning of the public economy in Los Angeles County has been described as the "institutionalization of competition." [19] Virtually no governmental unit holds legal monopoly positions (which is the same as saying there is tremendous overlapping of political units with authority to undertake provision of public goods and services) and, especially in the contract cities, there are skilled representatives of consumers as well as producers. The brief description in this study indicates what other observers feel to be the important characteristics of the developing public economy in a large and rapidly grow-

[19] Warren, *Government in Metropolitan Regions,* chs. 12 and 13.

ing urban area; dynamism, competition, and change taking place within an understandable system geared to efficient meeting of consumer demands. The large number of units do interact in a systematic manner and definitely do not constitute a chaotic and uncontrollable situation.

This is not to indicate that there are no problems in Los Angeles County. There are problems, and they may be classified into two groups: first, those affecting citizens where demand articulation mechanisms are lacking, and, second, the problems of area-wide coordination.

Groups of citizens that lack demand articulating mechanisms are found predominantly in communities or neighborhoods having preferences different from the rest of the city. Many of these neighborhoods are within the City of Los Angeles and are largely subject to the monopoly power of the city administration. For example, people in Watts and Hollywood have preferences for public goods and services that differ from those of the majority of citizens in Los Angeles. Watts and Hollywood (and many other areas) are, however, political nonentities with no formal mechanism for making their requirements felt in the city's political system. Administrative bureaucracies may and do make accommodations to differentiated demands—but usually, it is in response to the demands of high-income and knowledgeable persons, not to demands of minorities, especially low-income Blacks or Mexican Americans. For example, while big city school systems allegedly provide equal services within the city, superior services are normally furnished in high-income neighborhoods and poor services are found in low-income neighborhoods.[20] The neglect of Watts by the City of Los Angeles is now well known,[21] but it is not the only subarea within the monopolistic

[20] Jesse Burkhead, *Input and Output in Large-City High Schools* (Syracuse, N. Y.: Syracuse University Press, 1967), pp. 35–36.

[21] A survey following the Watts riots in 1965, comparing educational achievement and facilities of high-income areas of Pacific Palisades, Westwood and Brentwood with low-income areas of Watts and Avalon (primarily Black areas) and Boyle Heights and East Los Angeles (primarily Mexican-American areas), indicated inequalities in regard to the incidence of double sessions, cafeterias, libraries, and academically oriented course offerings. *Violence in the City—An End or a Beginning?* (Los Angeles: Governor's Commission on the Los Angeles Riots, December 2, 1965), pp. 49–61. This report is popularly known as the McCone Report, after its chairman, John A. McCone.

jurisdiction of the big city where citizen preferences are not met. The problem of articulation of demands by neighborhoods within big systems, and optimal production agencies, has yet to be solved in Los Angeles, as in most other big cities in the country.

The second problem occurs where area-wide cooperation would provide net gains but result in net losses for some areas. The many independent municipalities in Los Angeles County have considerable power to prevent bearing costs imposed by other units of government. For instance, a city can usually prevent the construction of a through freeway that will predominantly benefit users on either side of the city rather than the citizens in areas through which it passes. This poses an economic problem whenever potential net gains would be sufficient to compensate losers but there is no mechanism to implement such compensation. This is not the same problem stated by area-wide planners who say that the public interest is being thwarted by local political units, because in that case, the planners, not the citizens, are making a value comparison between gainers and losers, and planners may wish to impose their own preferences. The problems of relative gains and losses among political units have not been solved in either big-city systems or in polycentric systems such as Los Angeles. Within the big city systems, the high-income neighborhoods can usually prevent the imposition of costs on themselves, but low-income neighborhoods seem to be ideal places for highway construction and the like. These problems are serious. They have not been solved within single political units and are not going to be solved in polycentric political systems by granting monopoly power to some inclusive larger unit. In fact, one would predict that small political units do not seek solutions by giving up some of their power to larger units because they expect that consequent political externality costs would exceed net benefits and result in more serious big-unit problems. The observation that communities will cooperate on an area-wide basis when all parties benefit, either from the action itself or from compensation by gainers to losers from the action, is an indication that the polycentric system is capable of dealing with area-wide problems as well as meeting the demands of relatively small homogeneous groups within it—through cooperative effort for mutual gain rather than through an imposed political solution by some outside unit.

THE MIAMI–DADE COUNTY AREA

Miami-Dade County is not one of the largest metropolitan areas in the United States, but its governmental structure is interesting because of the transfer of a number of municipal functions to the county government in 1957. By this device, the county is permitted to undertake the provision of municipal-type services within municipalities without the consent of the municipality involved as well as within unincorporated areas of the county. This transfer of authority has been viewed as a way of handling area-wide problems on an area-wide scale, while leaving certain authority to the individual municipalities.

Evaluative research on the ability of the Miami-Dade County governmental structure to meet citizen demands is virtually nonexistent, both because of the difficulty of measuring either citizen demands or the outputs of the public goods and services and because few researchers have focused on that particular question. Descriptive information and an evaluative interpretation based on political reform preferences provide some indication as to how the system was created and how it functions. Existing data will be interpreted in the context of this analysis. The presentation will be divided into four parts: first, a description of the Dade County area; second, a discussion of the political system and functional coordination existing prior to creation of the new government; third, a discussion of the new governmental structure and what some of the problems appear to indicate; and, finally, an interpretation of the experiment in relation to other metropolitan areas of the United States.

Socioeconomic and Political Characteristics of Dade County

The 1970 population estimate of Dade County was 1,259,176 in an area of 2040 square miles (two-thirds of which is everglades), making it about one-half as large and one-sixth as populous as Los Angeles County.[22] Dade County's total population is less than half the population of the City of Los Angeles. The county contains thirty-six political units, thirty-three of which have property-taxing power.[23] Of the units, twenty-seven are municipalities, Miami being the largest with 332,000

[22] U.S. Bureau of the Census, "1970 Census of Population, Preliminary Reports," Series PC (P2)-124, Miami, Florida; Population Counts for Standard Metropolitan Statistical Areas, August, 1970.

[23] U.S. Bureau of the Census, Census of Governments, 1967.

people and two others, Hialeah and Miami Beach, having populations larger than 50,000. Eight cities are smaller than 1000. There are eight single-function districts, of which four are for water supply, three for housing and urban renewal, and one is the county-wide school district. There are also thirty-five subordinate special taxing areas managed by the county government.

Dade County is a rapidly growing area with most of its growth taking place since the 1920s, apparently largely because of the desirable climate. The population of the area shifts around and exhibits a large turnover; Miami itself does not appear to have stable internal population cleavages that characterize many large cities.[24] Some differentiated areas exhibiting socioeconomic characteristics different from the county population as a whole are found within the county, however. With one exception, these areas have resisted the imposition of county-wide political preferences on themselves. The main differentiated areas are the cities of Miami Beach, Hialeah, Coral Gables, and Homestead.[25]

Miami Beach. With a 1960 population of 63,145, Miami Beach has been described as the most homogeneous subcenter in the county, possessing a cohesive economic and social pattern. It is primarily a winter-haven and retirement home for the wealthy and has a large Jewish population. Composed of 7 percent of the county's population, it contains 20 percent of the assessed valuation.

Hialeah. This is primarily a working-class community, with a 1960 population of 66,972. It has an extremely low property tax base on residential property because of the homestead exemption,[26] but it contained 15.3 percent of the county's manufacturing in 1957 and was the location of over 31 percent of all new manufacturing in the county (three times as much as the City of Miami).

Coral Gables. Primarily an upper-class residential community, Coral Gables has a population of 34,793 and is the location of the University

[24] Wolff, *Miami Metro,* p. 77.

[25] *Ibid.,* pp. 62–67; Sofen, *Miami Metropolitan Experiment,* pp. 13–14.

[26] The Florida Homestead Exemption Law allows resident homeowners an exemption from taxation of $5,000 of assessed value of the property. Florida, *Constitution* (1885), Art. X, sec. 7. Essentially, this eliminates low-valued residences from property taxation.

of Miami. Professors who teach there describe it as the cultural center of the area.

Homestead. The 9,152 residents of Homestead live in the southern rural fringe of the county. Relatively homogeneous, the community was not considered part of the metropolitan area until the middle 1950s. It is a gateway to Everglades National Park and serves as a residence for some Air Force personnel.

Other subunits, such as Miami Springs and Miami Shores, show fairly identifiable characteristics, but the preceding four appear to be the most homogeneous and are most strongly differentiated from the rest of the metropolitan area.

Pre-1957 Functional Coordination

Functional coordination existed in Dade County, as in all other metropolitan areas, before the adoption of the new charter. While intergovernmental relations were not as extensive or complex as in Los Angeles County, contracting did take place, especially in the areas of water supply and police communications, cooperative agreements for fire protection, and delegation to county-wide government of the responsibility for provision of education, hospital, and jail services, and of a port authority with concern for both seaports and airports. County responsibility for hospitals and ports appears to be a consequence of Miami's abdication of county-wide political leadership during the depression when Miami was virtually bankrupt and unable to continue or expand its activities.[27]

The development of contractual relations may have been restricted somewhat by the lack of home-rule provisions for Florida municipalities. The state legislature has not permitted the municipalities, special districts, and counties to pursue advantageous functional coordination independently and, even now, its approval is required for any changes in the governmental structure of Dade County.

Consolidation of the ten school districts in the county into one county-wide system in 1945 was a rather unusual occurrence. Of the ten districts, only one, Miami Beach, had boundaries coinciding with municipal boundaries. Instead, the school boundaries had been drawn to follow township and section lines without regard for the existence of

[27] Wolff, *Miami Metro*, pp. 52–54.

communities or cities. The consolidation was approved by the state legislature and passed by the voters in the county, with the only opposition coming from Miami Beach because its school system was better than average and its property valuation higher than average. It is generally felt that, since consolidation, the county school system has been able to raise the level of education county-wide enough to satisfy the demands even of Miami Beach for a high level of educational services, even though that municipality does contribute substantially to provision of the high level of education throughout the rest of the county.[28]

Adoption of a Home-Rule County Charter

There were several attempts at consolidation of governmental units in Dade County prior to the adoption of the County Home-Rule Charter in 1957. The groundwork for the new charter itself required about four years, during which the state legislature passed an essential state constitutional amendment authorizing the drafting of the charter. The effect of the amendment and charter was to allow the citizens of Dade County to regulate their own local affairs, including setting the rules for incorporations, boundary adjustments, and abolition of municipalities and other political units within the county. Both the county and its municipalities were now freed from having to go to the state legislature for the enactment of local laws, and the voters in Dade County were permitted to establish a metropolitan government if they so desired.

The adoption of this amendment to the Florida State Constitution opened the door for considerable change in the structure and functioning of local government units with the consent of a little more than 50 percent of the voters. No provisions were made for single municipalities or for groups of people to veto the imposition of political externality costs on themselves by a majority of the county as a whole.

Following adoption of the amendment, a Charter Commission was created to write a charter for Dade County for presentation to the voters. The commission immediately adopted a position that the "autonomy" of the municipalities would be preserved for purely local functions and that no municipalities would be abolished. The issues then became essentially (1) the division of functions into those of a purely local character and those of county-wide importance, and (2) the delineation of limits that should be placed on the new county government. Some differences cropped up in distinguishing area-wide and local jurisdiction, but

[28] *Ibid.*, pp. 111–114.

this conflict appears to have been unimportant in writing up the charter
—and, like most charters, this document was ambiguous in many specific instances. Because a detailed examination of the charter provisions is
available elsewhere, only a few points need be made here.[29] First, the
county was authorized to set minimum standards for all types of services
and had power to take over operation of those services within a municipality if the minimum standards were not met. Second, the county was
given exclusive jurisdiction over unincorporated areas.

The charter was adopted in a county-wide vote of 44,404 to 42,620,
with 26 percent of Dade County's registered voters going to the polls
May 21, 1957. In general, it is not hard to pinpoint the sources of
opposition—they would have been expected to be municipalities whose
socioeconomic characteristics and demands for public goods and services
were different than the county's as a whole. This was, in fact, the case—
with one major exception. Not a single precinct in Miami Beach or
Hialeah, the second and third largest cities in the county, voted in favor
of the charter. Other cities, such as Homestead (in the rural south),
Miami Shores, and Miami Springs, also voted "no." The charter passed
because of extremely strong support in the City of Miami and in Coral
Gables. The unincorporated areas of the county disapproved by a nar-
row margin. The only surprising vote was that of Coral Gables which,
because its socioeconomic level was higher than the county average,
would have been expected to desire some autonomy. On the other hand,
and in retrospect, it is also the home of the University of Miami and
may have exhibited a strong political reform ideology.

The major controversies over division of functions between local and
county jurisdiction arose after adoption of the charter. Many of them
have been attributed to a "lack of leadership" [30] at the county level, but

---

[29] Sofen, *Miami Metropolitan Experiment,* pp. 50–58.

[30] Part of the lack of leadership may be related to the at-large elections
for county commissioners, which prevents any elected political official from
building a political base to respond to interests of individuals in a particular
geographic area. The at-large election system was promoted in 1963 by the
major newspapers and downtown businessmen specifically to prevent the
buildup of any strong geographically based political organization. This, combined with lack of a strong party system in Florida, of course, gives the newspapers a major voice in the political system. Thomas J. Wood, "Dade
County: Unbossed, Erratically Led," *The Annals,* CCCLIII (May 1964), 64–
71. See also Sofen, *Miami Metropolitan Experiment,* ch. 18.

one may suspect that any subunits in the county having strongly dif-- ferentiated demands for government goods and services would provide a source of instability unless those diverse demands could be attained. The instability and the dissatisfaction with which some municipalities viewed the strong county government were illustrated by the county-wide vote on the autonomy amendment in 1958; again, Miami Beach, Hialeah, Homestead, and some other cities registered strong approval of guaranteeing increased autonomy to the municipalities. Negative votes from Miami, Coral Gables, and the unincorporated areas defeated the amendment. Several other county-wide votes characterized as pro- or anti-"metro" have shown a consistent pattern of anti-metroism by Miami Beach, Hialeah, and Homestead, but these subsequent issues do not appear to have a direct bearing on county-municipality divisions of responsibilities.

The votes are not the only indication that some cities are dissatisfied with the present governmental structure. Miami Beach resisted the *lowering* of its building code requirements to county-wide uniform standards because its large number of tourists and potential tropical storm damage made higher standards advisable. The municipality even went so far as to pass a city council resolution to secede from Dade County.

In 1958 and 1959, the county commissioners did pass legislation permitting formation of special districts within the county and the creation of special taxing districts in unincorporated areas to facilitate dealing with localized problems on less than a county-wide basis.

The allocation of responsibilities between the county and its mu-nicipalities now appears to be near settlement, although not to the satis-faction of those communities with demands that are different from the rest of the county's; at present, the major problem appears to be financ-ing the county government. The current county property tax is levied at uniform county-wide rates in both unincorporated and incorporated areas; in the former, it is used to finance urban-type public services that are financed by municipal taxes in the municipalities. It is unlikely that this subsidization for citizens in unincorporated areas will continue for-ever; but the possibility does exist because the population is increasing most rapidly in unincorporated areas and, since municipal powers are limited and present financial arrangements favor unincorporated areas, there are no strong incentives for incorporation. On the contrary, the

City of Miami has made efforts at unincorporating and simply merging with the county.[31]

Conclusions on Miami–Dade County

The research done so far on Dade County does not permit an evaluation of the efficiency of the public economy in meeting citizen demands. No concerted attempts have been made to find more efficient producers or to cost out and measure government goods and services, as in Los Angeles County. If anything, potential competition is being eliminated for the monopoly positions of the county in areas where functions are classed as county-wide. There are no a priori reasons why a monopoly structure would be expected to be more efficient than a polycentric competitive structure where cooperation is based on voluntary consent and a search for the most efficient methods. But this question requires empirical evidence that would include both costs and measures of benefits of public services—measurements that are seldom undertaken, let alone available at present for either Dade County or Los Angeles County.

There are some a priori reasons, however, to expect that citizens with either higher or lower demands for public services will encounter difficulties in getting the public sector to respond to their demands, and this may provide a continuing source of instability for the Dade County public sector. On the other hand, citizens whose demands are close to average are likely to be satisfied with the present structure—especially those living in unincorporated areas that are subsidized by property taxes from wealthier incorporated municipalities. It will be interesting to follow the future development of Dade County to see how it responds to accommodating the diverse demands of some of its citizens and how it resolves the present financial problem of subsidizing citizens in unincorporated areas.

CONCLUSIONS

Two quite different metropolitan public economies have been examined, one having nearly seven million people and an extremely complex structure of political units and interaction and the other having one million population and a fairly simple political structure. Both represent attempts

[31] Sofen, *Miami Metropolitan Experiment,* pp. 101–105.

to organize the political structure to achieve some desired state of affairs. Data are not available to evaluate just what has been achieved—or how efficiently. However, some comparisons within the framework of the individualistic model developed in Chapter 3 of this study are possible. While any conclusions are severely limited, such a comparison does offer a chance for examining metropolitan area political systems within a somewhat different framework.

Social Interaction Costs

Chapter 3 discussed the costs of decision-making and of political externalities, along with techniques for reducing these social interaction costs by adjusting decision-making rules and using delegation and political leadership. It was noted that a tradeoff is likely between decision-making costs and political externality costs as well as between the size and scope of political units and the potential impact of a single vote on policy outcomes. A casual look at the Los Angeles County political structure would indicate that, because of the complexity of the structure and the veto power of many small independent units, decision-making costs would be quite high while, on the other hand, a citizen could minimize the cost of political externalities by residing in a relatively homogeneous unit. Since Miami contains a simple structure, domination of the county over the municipalities would lead citizens to expect relatively low decision-making costs; if their tastes should differ from the average, they might expect potentially high political externalities, especially in view of the lack of correlation between taxation and benefits received.

The two sets of expectations may be realized. However, Los Angeles County has innovated an arrangement whereby cities contract for public goods and services through the office of a city administrator who is primarily concerned with satisfying citizen preferences and uses his professional skills to seek the best methods of providing for citizen demands at the lowest costs. This may serve to lower decision-making costs and provide both lower costs and lower political externalities than in Dade County. On the other hand, it may be that, while a citizen of the City of Los Angeles enjoys low decision-making costs, he also faces the possibility of receiving very few benefits from the city provision of public goods and services, and he may be forced to bear heavy political externalities. In many ways, the City of Los Angeles with its essentially monopolistic powers, resembles Dade County more than the two counties resemble one another.

Articulation of Demand

Both the City of Los Angeles and Dade County appear unresponsive to the demands of citizens having either higher or lower preferences for public goods and services. However, the individual cities within Los Angeles County, with their homogeneous groupings of citizens, seem able to reflect demand quite efficiently.

Supply Conditions and Economies of Scale

Little can be said about economies of scale. Economic studies have not identified the potential decrease in average costs for virtually all public goods and services for populations beyond 100,000, and both Dade County and Los Angeles County have adequate population to achieve any such economies. The much more extensive division of demand articulation from production of supply and the competitive bidding to supply services in Los Angeles County's contract cities would indicate that the decentralized system can adjust both to achieve economies of scale and to provide incentives for efficient production. It is unclear whether any incentives to encourage a search for increased efficiency in the production of public goods and services exist in the monopolistic structures of Dade County or whether county-wide production is most efficient for all county-wide services.

Flexibility and the Maintenance of Options

Maintenance of options for the satisfaction of demands for public goods and services is unquestionably superior in contract cities in Los Angeles. Separation of demand-articulation units from producing units permits changes in sources of supply in response to any changes in technical conditions that would make a larger or smaller unit more efficient. Dade County and Los Angeles City, on the other hand, are restricted by the integration of their demand and supply functions in making adjustments in supply conditions in response to technical change. Since future conditions are always uncertain, the flexibility of the Los Angeles contract-city system may be its most important attribute.

These cursory conclusions are not based on hard evidence, but on implications arising from economic assumptions that individuals rationally seek their own self-interest, that knowledge is scarce and expensive, and that some types of economic goods have externalities or are of a public goods nature. It is not unexpected that implications drawn from these assumptions differ from conclusions of perfect-knowledge, Philosopher-King models. What is interesting, however, is the close resemblance of the Los Angeles County public economy (outside the City of Los Angeles) to a theoretically efficient structure and the strong deviations of the Dade County public economy when it is represented as the model of government for the future. The Dade County model is not completely unpredictable, however; in a decision-making structure that permits a 50 percent vote in a large and relatively undifferentiated area to determine that area's organization, one would expect that decision-making costs would be reduced for the majority—even if demands of different minorities were ignored, as appears to be the case in Dade County.

Hopefully, the conclusions drawn here will stimulate further empirical investigation to determine how efficiently the different public economies do function to meet citizen demands (or planner preferences, if political reformers insist), especially since the theoretical implications of this analysis are so much at variance with many currently accepted conclusions concerning efficient organization of the public economy in metropolitan areas.

Chapter 6

FUNCTIONAL AREA ANALYSIS: EDUCATION AND AIR POLLUTION CONTROL

INTRODUCTION

Two functional areas of public activity—education and air pollution control—have been selected to illustrate the applicability of the theoretical framework developed in Chapters 1–3 to an understanding of the functioning of the public economy. Education was selected because it involves the largest expenditures of state and local government and because recent research by both economists and noneconomists provides empirical data of sufficient quantity and quality upon which to base an analysis of this type. As will be seen, the demand and provision of education also involve questions of externalities, public goods, boundaries, economies of scale, demand articulation, and financing—all the considerations one could ask for in analyzing a public good or service.

Air pollution control is a relatively small activity of government, but with other environmental controls, it is likely to become increasingly important in the future. In the form of smoke, air pollution represents one of the classic examples of external diseconomies not dealt with in private market relationships. Air pollution control also presents problems of externalities, public goods, boundaries and property rights, although it provides a somewhat simpler example of the provision of a public good than does education. Both activities, however, are amenable to application of the theory of public goods and provide some evidence (or, at the very least, do not refute the hypothesis) that the American public economy functions like the model constructed in Chapters 2 and

3. As with the examination of governmental organization, the analysis of education and air pollution control illustrates the applicability of the theoretical framework; it is not a complete analysis of the functions.

EDUCATION

Education is the largest component of the domestic American public economy. In 1969, public school expenditures for elementary and secondary education totaled $28.6 billion. Some 23,390 public school systems operated 91,930 schools with an enrollment of 45,624,000 students. In addition, 6.3 million students attended 19,000 private elementary and secondary schools. Expenditure per pupil ranged from $1,140 in New York to $432 in Alabama, with an average of $696 for the entire United States.[1]

Of many possible ways to examine education, the method here is, first, to analyze components of the demand for education by looking at (1) the benefits from education, (2) how demand is articulated, and (3) how the provision of education is financed. Following the analysis of demand, a brief analysis of production will focus on some apparent problems.

The Demand for Education

Examination of the demand for education leads to several problems not found in the examination of demand for a privately consumed good. The consumer of a private good precisely indicates his effective demand (which reflects his benefits) by purchasing some quantity of the good. Thus, identification of effective demand, benefit, and financing are identifiable from a single transaction. With a public good or service, the relationships are not so simple. First, by definition, the value of benefits is equal to effective demand—that is, the amount of resources a po-

[1] Expenditure and student data from U.S. Department of Health, Education and Welfare, *Digest of Educational Statistics, 1969* (Washington, D.C.: U.S. Government Printing Office, 1969), Tables 25, 70, 74; school and school system data from U.S. Bureau of the Census, *Census of Governments, 1967*, Vol. 1, "Governmental Organization," (Washington, D.C.: U.S. Government Printing Office, 1968), p. 6; private school data from U.S. Bureau of the Census, *Statistical Abstract of the United States, 1969* (Washington, D.C.: U.S. Government Printing Office, 1969), Tables 140, 141.

tential demander is willing to give up in order to obtain the public good. But an individual who will benefit and does have an effective demand would find it to his advantage to understate his demands and become a free-rider, if financing is based on voluntary payment. To resolve the free-rider problem, the public good is provided through a political unit in which each individual knows that he and everyone else must share costs for the amount of the good they want provided; thus, any single individual is likely to express just how much of the good he desires, because he knows that his final contribution will be decided on the basis of aggregated community preferences, rather than on his own statement of demands. The approach to identifying the effective demand for education, then, will be to examine who benefits from the provision and consumption of education, how demands are articulated, and how financing is provided.

Benefits from Education. Werner Hirsch is one of several economists who have provided categories of educational benefits.[2] While other analysts may prefer different categories for different purposes, Hirsch's classifications are quite satisfactory for use here. They comprise direct and indirect benefits and short- and long-run benefits. Direct benefits are those accruing to the student and/or his family as a result of the student's consumption of education. Indirect benefits accrue to individuals and families as a result of *other* students' consumption of education. Short-run benefits are achieved simultaneously with the consumption of education. Long-run benefits accrue in the future, often after the consumption of education is completed. Benefits from education are:

A. Long-Run Direct Benefits
   1. Increased productivity of the individual because of his education (likely to accrue as increased monetary income).
   2. Increased satisfaction and cultural benefits (as psychic rather than monetary income).
B. Short-Run Direct Benefits

[2] Werner Z. Hirsch, Elbert W. Segelhorst, and Morton J. Marcus, *Spillover of Public Education Costs and Benefits* (Los Angeles: University of California, Institute of Government and Public Affairs, 1964). Also see Burton A. Weisbrod, *External Benefits of Public Education* (Princeton, N.J.: Princeton University, Industrial Relations Section, Department of Economics, 1964).

    1. Benefits accruing to the family because of school custody of the child during the day (may accrue as monetary income if mother chooses to work, or as psychic income if she is free to undertake other activities).

    2. Consumption benefits of the students (with compulsory education, short-run benefits could be negative—that is, the student and his family would be better off if the student did something else, such as farm work).

C. Indirect Long-Run Benefits

    1. Benefits from the increased productivity of other individuals accrue as:

        reduced taxes or increased public goods as the result of higher taxable incomes of other citizens;

        reduced burdens of social-welfare expenditure and resultant lower taxes;

        decreased education and training costs to employers (possibly passed on to consumers);

        positive externalities (or reduced negative externalities) from improved living conditions of neighbors.

    2. Benefits consequent on higher cultural levels of other citizens accrue as:

        reduced future costs of education because of informal education in students' homes;

        improved living conditions of neighbors;

        growth of an informed and literate electorate;

        reduced interaction costs—both decision-making costs and political externality costs—to the extent that a common educational experience produces similar tastes, permitting the public economy to function more efficiently.

D. Indirect Short-Run Benefits

    Benefits from the increased productivity of mothers freed from custodial care of their children accrue as reduced taxes or increased public goods for non-student families resulting from the income of students' working mothers.

Both direct and indirect benefits listed indicate that individuals (or families) are likely to have a demand for the education both of their own and of other people's children, and the demand for the education of other people's children (which may also be characterized as a demand for a literate and well-educated society) is very much a public good, in that additional persons consume the benefits of the existence of such a society without reducing its consumption by other individuals. Thus, education may be characterized as simultaneously possessing the qualities of both private and public goods—perhaps, more specifically, as a private good offering external benefits in the nature of a public good to other citizens in society.

The provision of a free public school system that is available to each citizen provides benefits that may be considered a response to option demand, but it appears to be more than that. The public school movement seems to be strongly rooted in the concept that any child may receive a free education and, thus, share in the opportunities of the American way of life; if this is the case, some of the demand for a literate and well-educated society could include this special aspect of education as a demand for opportunities for all American children.

The identification of magnitudes of educational benefits that accrue as public goods requires the introduction of spatial relations and boundary problems. This is required for two reasons: first, since individuals educated in one community will often migrate to other communities, the long-run indirect benefits of their education will accrue to the new community rather than to the one providing the education; second, even without migration, benefits and costs will accrue in different degrees at different distances from the community providing the education. For instance, reduction of taxes resulting from increased earning power of any given citizen may accrue to the entire nation, to the state, the county, the city, etc., depending on the taxing system in effect, while reduced costs of future education attributable to informal education provided by educated parents in the home are likely to accrue pretty much to the local community.

In an attempt to identify benefits from education and the area to which they accrue, Hirsch made a detailed examination of Clayton School District in Missouri. He concluded that the citizens of Clayton School District received 78.1 percent of the benefits generated by their provision of education, residents of the St. Louis Standard Metropolitan Statistical Area outside the Clayton District received 1.3 percent, while all other Missouri citizens received 1.2 percent and U. S. citizens outside this area received 19.4 percent.[3] The relatively large share of benefits accruing to the rest of the United States is due to the federal income tax which

[3] Hirsch, et al., *Spill-over*, p. 355.

captures a share of increased incomes from individuals educated in the Clayton system.[4]

On the basis of a similar analysis, Weisbrod concluded that when benefits accrue outside of the school district (that is, positive external effects), education tends to be underprovided, because spillins are taken as a given factor and costs equated with local benefits.[5] This conclusion is incorrect, however. As will be seen in an analysis of financing, because costs, as well as benefits, are often spilled out, local costs are less than total costs, just as local benefits are less than total benefits.

Demand Articulation. Education in the United States has been provided primarily by local school districts. Within these districts, demand is articulated by citizens in a variety of ways, including direct voting on some issues, voting for delegates who, in turn, decide educational policy, and directly confronting educators (administrators and teachers) either individually or in groups, such as the PTA, or, perhaps, by other means. If Hirsch's estimates are accurate and Clayton is fairly representative, citizens' demands for locally provided education probably constitute the major share of their demand for education—probably all of that for one's own children and most of that for other people's children. Thus, the local school districts serve as a mechanism for both the articulation of demand and provision of supply of public education.[6] This mechanism is more complex, however, when demands for education outside the local school district are taken into account. It is useful to treat the articulation of demands by individuals for local education and for education outside the local school district separately.

First, demands for local education vary in the same way as do demands for other public and private goods and services. Within a single local school district, the level and kind of education provided is likely to reflect the median preferences of the community; this is likely to meet individual demands most closely if individuals have similar demands for education. If the community is not homogeneous, however, citizens with either higher, lower, or different demands are likely to seek alternative educational opportunities. Alternatives may be sought by (1) trying to influence the level and kind of education provided

[4] This abstracts from any analysis of federal expenditure incidence.

[5] Weisbrod, *External Benefits,* p. 121.

[6] Contracting is done by some 2,000 school districts (called nonoperating) that send their students to neighboring districts.

locally, (2) moving to another public school district where education more nearly meets demands, or (3) purchasing education from a private school. However, these options may not be available on an equal basis.

Low-income individuals who feel that their tax share is high relative to their demands (even though a large part of their education is subsidized by other citizens who have higher incomes because low-income families are unable to bear the full costs of providing the education) may be severely limited in the exercise of options—their political influence may be nil, their residential mobility restricted, and their incomes insufficient to educate their children in private schools. Children with low educational demands, or with demands for a mix of services not provided in the local public schools are likely to have two choices—attend school, even though it is less than satisfactory, or simply drop out. One must remember that the opportunity costs of attending school fall heavily on the individual involved; unless the benefits of school attendance exceed these costs, the individual would benefit from dropping out of school and seeking other opportunities. The high dropout rates (and difficulty of reentry) in many school districts, especially the big cities, would indicate a priori that many school districts are not providing a level or mix of educational services to meet the demands of large proportions of their potential clientele.

High-income individuals and families who feel their demands are higher than local provision are likely to have several opportunities to influence their educational consumption. High-income families, presumably exerting more political power than low-income families, may be able to influence the level or type of education provided locally; they are also likely to have the resources and capability to move to an area where families have similar tastes and the median level of education provided is closer to their demands; and, third, they may have sufficient resources to pay for private school educational services even though, as a member of the local political unit, they must pay for public education as well.

It appears that within the larger single-school systems, adjustments in the provision of educational services accommodate the diverse demands of different neighborhoods—especially demands in high-income neighborhoods. For instance, one finds higher levels of education provided in high-income neighborhoods, as teachers with seniority gravitate toward the "more desirable" schools in the system—usually defined as schools with student populations having socioeconomic characteristics similar to those of the teachers themselves. The low-income area schools, on the other hand, are likely to have an extremely high teacher turnover and to be neglected in other ways by the educational administrative bureaucracy. Even with these adjustments, however, it appears that many large-city school systems are not satisfactorily accommodating those citizens with either extremely high, extremely low, or different demands. The result is a high rate of low-income and low-demand dropouts and an exodus to the suburbs or use of private schools by high-demand families. The failure of large-city educational systems to adjust to the demands of individuals with high demands for local education may be a significantly contributing factor to the migration of high-income families from the large central cities in the United States. The difficulties of adjustment to citizen demands in large-city school systems are considered in greater detail along with the provision of education.

Local citizens demand not only locally provided education, but education outside of the local districts because of anticipated spillovers. This demand for education outside the local unit may be taken into account in any of several ways, and, to some extent, the methods used will depend on the assignment of property rights; that is, do citizens have the right to force others to educate their children to prevent negative spillovers (associated with low education) to the rest of the country, or should citizens pay for the provision of education elsewhere because they receive positive spillover benefits from that education?

One approach would be to say that people started out uneducated and that beneficiaries from their education should pay for the benefits; thus, some payments from local districts could be made to other districts to reflect the benefits a local district receives. This would result in a lot of transfers between the different districts, perhaps netting out at zero for many of them. The process would also probably entail high bargaining costs among districts.

A second approach would be to assign a property right to every local district, stating that no other district could impose negative externalities (or foregone benefits) by failure to educate its children to a certain level. Thus, one would be legislating minimum standards applicable to all districts, perhaps forcing some of them to provide more education than they would otherwise have done, but enabling each of them to receive benefits from education provided in other districts and paid for by other districts. This would eliminate transfers among districts, and decision-making costs would probably be lower than in the case where beneficiaries pay directly for all benefits received. A third method of dealing with spillovers would be to enlarge the local unit to include all persons affected by educational spillovers—perhaps the entire country, or perhaps the continent, or the whole world. For reasons presented in Chapter 3, however, since efforts to internalize all externalities within a single hierarchical framework usually involve increased costs, this approach may not be feasible.

A fourth approach would be to form an organization encompassing many local school districts to deal with spillovers between units, much as local school districts, as a political unit, deal with spillovers among individuals within the unit. If some units encompass many school districts, these might be utilized more efficiently than starting up a completely new unit. The logical units for dealing with school district spillovers are the county, state, and national governments; the units that do deal, for the most part, with spillovers of local school districts are state and the national governments. The larger political unit, then, becomes a representative of all the units and citizens within its jurisdiction in dealing with the local school district, and we are back to the basic two-party bargaining situation examined in Figure 2-1, where the local unit is one party and the larger unit is the other.

A local/nonlocal educational spillover situation is illustrated in Figure 6-1. MG represents the sum of marginal benefits (and hence demands) from local individuals for locally provided education. DC represents the sum of marginal benefits (and hence demands) by nonlocal individuals for educational benefits that spill out of the local area. The sum of local and nonlocal demands is PG. The marginal cost of production of education is assumed constant and illustrated by IL.

If only local demands were taken into account, the equilibrium output would be A, where local marginal benefits (AJ) equal marginal cost (also AJ). At A, however, total marginal benefits (AN) exceed marginal costs (AJ); thus, net gains could be made by expanding output. At optimal output (B), total marginal benefits to both locals and nonlocals (BK) are equal to marginal cost. At that output, total benefits are $OPKB$ and total costs are $OIKB$, with net benefits (IPK) maximized.

Output level B could be achieved in either of two ways: nonlocals could pay the local district to expand output from A to B or minimum standards of level B could be legislated by a larger political unit. If payment by nonlocals were used, the amount could range from a minimum equal to JKH (the amount by which costs exceed local bene-

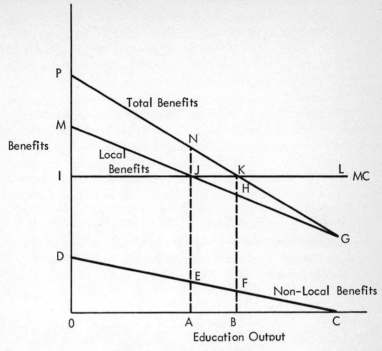

Figure 6-1. Education Spillovers

fits over range *AB*) to a maximum of *AEFB* (the total value of increased nonlocal benefits).

In the United States, both the legislation of minimum standards and payments by larger units (states and the national government) are used to influence the level of education provided by local school districts. Historically, states have relied on minimum standard legislation rather than on direct payments. However, increasing emphasis is being placed on equal opportunities, and some states are going to payments because it is recognized that some low-income districts are unable to provide a level of education that will not result in negative externalities (or foregone opportunities) to other areas. The national government has traditionally relied on payments, primarily for specialized functions such as vocational education, library resources, education for the handicapped, and basic adult education. Payment programs by both state and national governments are usually worked out through bargaining and contracted relationships, and the local unit is required to provide some increase in educational levels or some specific educational output for which the larger unit pays from tax revenues collected over the larger area. This provides for coordination of educational provision over large areas by bargaining between two or more parties as an alternative to internalizing all educational provision within a single organization.

One would expect that if citizens become more mobile and economic relationships increase over larger and larger areas of a country and economy, the provision of education would involve an increase in spillovers. This has been the case in the United States. Increasing pressure to finance part of the provision of educational services and to enforce minimum-level provisions, first at the state and now, at the national level, has accompanied these spillover effects. It appears likely that these trends will continue.

Financing. The third aspect of identifying demand for education is financing. Historically, education in the United States has been provided by local school districts for local citizens and financed by local property taxes. Because high-income individuals appear to have high demands for education and low-income individuals have relatively lower demands for education, the property tax, which is correlated with income and wealth, provides some adjustment of the tax price in relation to the intensity of demands for educational services.[7] This method of financing, however, does not allocate financing in direct relationship to benefits received. It neglects spillover problems and ignores differences between families with and without children (except to the extent that families with more children possess more property subject to taxation). The same tax treatment of families with and without children has been justified by the contention that education is equally available for all and that part of the benefits of education accrue indirectly to all citizens, rather than directly to the children and their families. Financing of spillover benefits has been adjusted by increasing the share of higher and more inclusive levels of government to supplement the local financing efforts. One important aspect of spillovers that has been ignored until very recently is

[7] Property taxes, while regressive, are correlated with income and wealth, as individuals with higher incomes pay higher absolute amounts of taxes. Education and income of parents (both highly correlated) are highly correlated with expenditures on education. James N. Morgan, et al., *Income and Welfare in the United States* (New York: McGraw-Hill, 1962), p. 383.

the spillover of taxes, as well as benefits, to individuals outside the local school district.

Use of the property tax for financing local education does result in part of the incidence of the tax being passed on to individuals who reside outside the local district but carry out economic transactions with businesses or industries located within the local school district. A large shopping center in a school district relieves the local residents of a tax burden because property taxes paid by the center derive, in part, from revenues of citizens who reside outside the local district but do some shopping within it. It is true, but less obvious, that the same result occurs when manufacturers in a district ship products outside the local district and pay local taxes from revenues obtained by the export sales.

Most local school districts have both tax spillouts and tax spillins (when their citizens purchase goods from outside the local area) as well as benefit spillouts and spillins. Mechanisms for adjusting tax spillovers are not as developed as those for benefit spillovers, but increased recognition of this aspect of providing education may lead to further attempts at adjustment. At present, however, the theoretical problems and information costs of identifying tax incidence preclude anything more than crude adjustments, since more rigorous attempts would probably cost more than the value of any benefits achievable from possessing the additional information.

Direct taxes for schools are not the only financing necessary for the provision of education. Municipal services such as police and fire protection, water and sewer facilities—all financed from general taxes—are usually provided without a direct charge to the school district. Analysis of costs of these services attributable to schools is virtually nonexistent, but the economic costs exist and may be important in some areas.

In studies of financing for the provision of education, only a crude balance has been struck between prices paid and benefits received. It is impossible to say, a priori, whether the divergence between benefit and burden results in underproduction or overproduction of educational services. Fortunately, there appears to be a high level of agreement that education must be available to all citizens and that it should be financed somewhat broadly, so that specific (and probably expensive) attempts at identifying costs and benefits have not been emphasized as much as the general benefits of a literate, well-educated society. It may be possible to increase the efficiency of meeting citizen demands for education and other public services, however, if knowledge is gained and institutions are adjusted to provide for a closer fit between benefits and costs of educational services, especially since this represents the largest area of state and local government expenditures.

The Supply of Education

Primarily, public education in the United States is provided by local school districts. Local districts construct or lease physical plants, hire instructors and administrators, purchase supplies, etc., to produce educational services for residents of the local district. Local districts exercise mutually exclusive monopolistic jurisdictions; within the districts, separate plants (schools) usually possess monopolistic jurisdiction over residents of specific geographic areas. The local school districts not only produce educational services but, in most cases, are the organizational unit through which local citizens can voice their demands for local education. Thus, the school district serves both to articulate local demands and to produce local supply as a monopolist in its area.

This unification of demand and production in a single monopolistic unit is largely a result of historical conditions. When education was first provided in America, population densities were generally so low that the production of education was a natural monopoly. There simply were not enough students within traveling distance to justify the operation of more than one school in a local area; in fact, population densities were sometimes so low that it was inefficient to provide more than a single classroom and a single teacher for several grades. As travel time decreased without a corresponding increase in population densities in rural areas, school districts tended to consolidate to gain the advantages of larger production plants. This was especially true at the high school level, where a variety of courses and programs can be offered efficiently only if there are large numbers of students. Even with consolidations, many rural school districts are unable to encompass a large enough area to achieve a varied offering of educational programs at reasonable cost.

In urbanizing areas, school districts have encountered a quite different problem. As population has increased within school district boundaries, the districts have simply built more plants, partitioning the geographic areas into smaller and smaller units. The process has produced many nearly identical plants, each with its own monopoly clientele, clustered in relatively small geographic areas. Some separation of functions has taken place in the larger school districts, where vocational shops were the first activity to be separated from other high schools in the system. This innovation has served to offer local students a choice of schools to attend without having to change residence or enroll in a private school.

Many attempts have been made to identify the relationships between the various inputs (such as teachers' time, materials, plant and equipment, and students' time) and outputs (such as increased skills of students).[8] Most of these attempts have been somewhat inconclusive or have identified the outputs, that is, skill achievements, as being primarily correlated with noninput variables, such as income or education of parents, rather than by educational inputs. Attempts to identify economies of scale have also been made. These have indicated decreasing costs for expansion of extremely small districts and increasing costs in extremely large districts. In general, however, the difficulties of measuring outputs from education have made identification of production functions quite difficult. Until production functions can be identified, it will be extremely difficult to evaluate efficiency in the production of education. It would also appear that as long as individual schools and school systems are monopolies, the incentives for increased efficiency in production and increased responsiveness to individual demands may be lacking. These issues are illustrated by a look at school systems with severe problems— big-city school systems—although smaller systems may have similar problems on a lesser scale.

Big–City School Systems

The process of simply creating additional plants within a system to handle increasing numbers of students without changing the size and structure of the school district has led to some acute and special problems in big-city school districts. New York City's system, with over

[8] For examples, see Jesse Burkhead, *Input and Output in Large-City High Schools* (Syracuse: Syracuse University Press, 1967); Herbert J. Kiesling, *High School Size and Cost Factors* (U.S. Department of Health, Education, and Welfare, 1968); *idem*, "Measuring a Local Government Service: A Study of School Districts in New York State," *The Review of Economics and Statistics*, XLIX (August 1967), 356–367; Werner Z. Hirsch, "Expenditure Implications of Metropolitan Growth and Consolidation," *The Review of Economics and Statistics*, XLI (August 1959), 232–241; John Riew, "Economies of Scale in High School Operation," *The Review of Economics and Statistics*, XLVIII (August 1966), 280–287.

1 million students enrolled in 1966 in nearly 2,000 schools, is an extreme example of a system that has exhausted any advantages of largeness. Many other big-city systems face comparable problems.[9] It may be useful to examine current problems in big systems with a hope of avoiding them as other areas increase in population.

Most observers feel that citizens in big-city systems have no way to articulate their demands for education. As Gittell has pointed out:

> Conclusions from different types of political analysis are quite similar. Each identifies an inability of the urban education system to respond to pressing demands made upon it. The circle of school decision-makers is apparently confined to the school professional and the school board, with restricted participation by others.[10]

The emphasis is on preserving the status quo—not on adjusting to change.

As pointed out in Chapter 3, one would expect difficulties in articulating diverse preferences into an extremely large system and should not be surprised that large bureaucracies are not very responsive.

In addition to the problems of size per se, when school districts have become too large for effective citizen control, they have proved vulnerable to virtual takeover by professional educators. Increased professionalization may, in fact, very well be a necessity for running any extremely large system. However, the lack of adaptability to diverse demands, and especially to new demands, is at best a reflection of bureaucratic inflexibility. In New York City, the failure of professionals to promote innovation is considered, not an accident, "but a reflection of their need to maintain the system which protects their interests." [11]

It is difficult to say much about the outputs of educational expenditures in New York City or other large systems, except that many citizens are dissatisfied with them. Most analyses of education measure *inputs,* such as dollars spent per pupil, student-teacher ratios, etc., rather than

[9] For example, see Marilyn Gittell and T. Edward Hollander, *Six Urban School Districts* (New York: Praeger, 1968) for an analysis of New York City, Philadelphia, Chicago, Detroit, St. Louis, and Baltimore.

[10] Marilyn Gittell, ed., *Educating an Urban Population* (Beverly Hills: Sage Publications, 1967), p. 10.

[11] Marilyn Gittell, "Decision-Making in the Schools: New York City, A Case Study," p. 231 in Marilyn Gittell, ed., *Educating an Urban Population.*

outputs, such as achievement. There may be, in fact, no direct relationship between expenditures and outputs if the school system is inefficient or if expenditures are made for outputs other than those demanded by the citizens and students.

The problems increasingly prevalent in big systems are predictable from the model developed in Chapters 2 and 3. The model also points out some potential innovations that would be expected to increase efficiency in meeting citizen demands for educational services. In discussing the conceptual division between demand-articulating units and producing units, it was noted that no special reason dictates that the unit articulating the demand should be the same as the unit providing the supply. Analysis of the Lakewood Plan contract cities of Los Angeles County in Chapter 6 showed a stream of benefits flowing from the division of these two functions. Milton Friedman and others have proposed a similar reform for education, aimed specifically at the present problem of suppliers who hold monopoly powers for the provision of education in specific geographic areas.[12] Friedman has suggested that parents of children be given certificates (or credit) for a specific amount of education, at least adequate to bring the student to an educational level where any negative externalities from his remaining uneducated will be removed and where he will be equipped to take advantage of opportunities in American society. The student and his family would then select the school he wishes to attend, and that school could be run privately, by a public body, or by any organization capable of running a school sufficiently attractive to be chosen by pupils and able to meet minimum standards of certification. In most urban areas, population densities are now such that most families would be within travel distance of several elementary schools and several high schools. The local community would determine the local tax revenue allocable to education while continuing to bargain with higher-level governments for increased revenues to be spent locally; more simply, minimum standards could be provided, with parents of children paying the increased costs of sending their children to higher-quality schools.[13]

[12] Milton Friedman, "The Role of Government in Education," in Robert A. Solow, ed., *Economics and the Public Interest* (New Brunswick, N.J.: Rutgers University Press, 1955), pp. 123–144.

[13] According to an article by Christopher Jencks in the July 4, 1970 *New Republic,* the Office of Economic Opportunity is preparing to fund an "Educational Voucher Agency" in a community to function essentially as Friedman

While Friedman's suggestion is somewhat radical, it would serve to meet the demands of citizens for the education of both their own and other people's children. By permitting parents a choice in selecting their school, it would break the monopoly power now held by school districts and would encourage schools to become more responsive to the demands of their citizens. Any schools not responsive or efficient enough to attract students would simply go out of business.

A different, and interesting, approach to improving educational efficiency in a big-city school system is presently being undertaken in Gary, Indiana. Gary has contracted with Behavioral Research Laboratories of Palo Alto, California, to run an elementary school in Gary for four years *on a money-back guaranteed-performance basis* for $800 per pupil, the amount Gary currently spends each year for elementary school students. Behavioral Research Laboratories guarantees to bring the achievement scores of the students up to the national norms for each grade, or at the end of three years refund to the city payments for any student who does not achieve national norms in all basic curriculum areas.[14] Contracting for the provision of education on a performance basis is comparable to the Lakewood Plan cities contracting for the provision of other goods and services, as examined in Chapter 5. It will be interesting to see the results of this experiment where the costs of failure to achieve certain educational standards will be shared by the educational producers as well as the students. If Behavioral Research Laboratories is successful, and additional firms are permitted to enter the education business in different cities, a potentially efficient and responsive competitive set of producers may provide educational services that will approximate citizen preferences more closely than existing school systems.

A less radical proposal than Friedman's or the experiment in Gary would be simply to break up excessively large systems. This should not be confused with attempts at internal decentralization—unless the central

---

has proposed. Programs similar to Friedman's are also being discussed seriously in academic and conference literature. See, for example, Anthony Downs, "Competition and Community Schools," in Henry M. Levin, ed., *Community Control of Schools* (Washington, D.C.: Brookings, 1970), pp. 219–249.

[14] "School City of Gary Contracts School to Educational Service Company on Money Back Guaranteed Performance Basis," Superintendent of Schools Office, School City of Gary, 620 East 10th Place, Gary, Indiana. July 22, 1970.

authority actually cedes power to the local units, decentralization is likely to be useless.[15] There is no reason why any area with sufficient population to achieve economies of scale in the operation of a school system should not be able to operate and to handle the boundary problems of spillovers with higher levels of political organization much as school districts do now. This would permit easier access by citizens to influencing the output of their local school system, thus reducing decision-making costs. To the extent that neighborhoods are somewhat homogeneous, it would be easier to meet the demands of that group of citizens in a single local system, while problems of equalization and minimum levels would continue to be dealt with by large, area-wide political units such as state and national governments.

Conclusions on Education

The public school system in the United States can be analyzed in terms of citizen demands and production of educational services, even though, providing education produces externalities that accrue in the nature of public goods. While the system can be analyzed in terms of the concepts developed in Chapters 2 and 3, it does appear that some systems, such as those in big cities, would not be classed as efficient organizational structures for articulating demand and producing educational services. Thus, to the extent that citizens are predicted to manage their affairs to create efficient institutional outputs, the model developed is not appropriate for positive analysis of the present state of big-city education.

One can predict, however, that the present conditions in big-city systems are not in equilibrium. To the extent that the model based on individual preferences has normative value, some of the suggestions for altering the institutional structure to resemble the model would improve its utility for the citizens who consume educational services in the big systems. At present, the professionals appear to have been able to take over the system and to run it as monopolists for their own, rather than for citizen, benefits. While the costs of reintroducing citizen influence on big-city school systems may be high, continuation of nonresponsive big systems with high student dropout rates may prove even more costly over the long run.

[15] Gittell and Hollander, *Six Urban School Districts*, pp. 64–76.

AIR POLLUTION CONTROL

Air pollution is the economist's classic example of an externality resulting from private market economic activity. It is only recently, however,
that air pollution appears to have become a relevant, and even Pareto-
relevant externality, where individuals are willing to pay to have pollution reduced in order to consume clean air. The economics of air pollution will be analyzed here to illustrate the applicability of the theoretical
framework, followed by an examination of some air pollution control
agencies and recent legislation to see how the problems of externalities,
public goods, collective action and boundaries between different political
units have been resolved. Although the treatment here is brief, it serves
to indicate the efficiency of the economic approach for a simple con-
ceptualization of what often appear, at first, to be complex problems.

The Economics of Pollution Control [16]

The use of air for disposal of smoke by a factory affords a simple
example of air pollution as an externality. In this case, the factory's costs
of production, if they were to reflect its total use of resources, must
include the damages imposed on nearby residents by smoke emission.
Those residents are likely to constitute a latent group—that is, while each
has a positive demand for less smoke, no individual demand is intense
enough to realize benefits to him in excess of the high cost of alleviating
the pollution.

Figure 6-2 shows demand and cost functions for a firm that emits
smoke in producing a product. The demand, or benefits to consumers
from the product, is line JF.[17] The cost of inputs purchased on the
market is CG. When the damages borne by recipients of air pollution
are added to market costs, total costs of production are CI. Without
considering pollution, the firm would produce output B, where its
marginal cost (BE) is equal to its marginal revenue, or price of the

[16] For a more detailed analysis of the issues presented in this section,
see Harold Wolozin, ed., *The Economics of Air Pollution* (New York:
Norton, 1966); Richard L. Stroup, "The Economics of Air Pollution Control," Ph.D. diss., Department of Economics, University of Washington,
Seattle, Washington, 1970.

[17] Demand is drawn as perfectly elastic to eliminate the problems of differences between marginal revenue and marginal benefits to consumers that
would only complicate, without adding anything to, the analysis.

product. At output B, however, total marginal costs, including pollution damages, are BK, an amount greater than marginal benefits by EK. Thus, the level of production is too high because the firm does not see the costs it imposes on others by its use of the airshed for disposal purposes. The economic efficiency problem is to get the firm to produce output A, where *total* marginal costs of AH equal marginal benefits, also AH. It is over the range of production AB that a Pareto-relevant externality exists, that is, the amount of damages borne by recipients ($DHKE$) is greater than the amount of benefits the firm gets from the additional output (DHE); thus, the firm and the recipients can be made better off (by amount HKE) from a reduction in output to A.

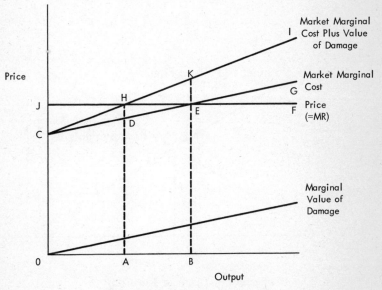

Figure 6-2. Firm with Externality

Figure 6-3 illustrates the firm and recipient situation in simplified form. MB represents the net marginal benefits to the firm for outputs up to B. The net marginal benefits are the difference between market costs and marginal revenue (price) in Figure 6-2; thus, OM in Figure 6-3 equals CJ in Figure 6-2 and AN in Figure 6-3 equals DH in Figure

6-2. At *B* in Figure 6-3, marginal net benefits are zero where the marginal revenue and market cost functions intersect at *E* in Figure 6-2. The damages to recipients of air pollution are shown by *OP* in Figure 6-3. They are zero at *O, AN* (equal to *HD*) at *A*, and *BP* (equal to *EK*) at *B*. The logic of the equilibrium situation, output *A*, was discussed in Figure 2-1 as the only place where the value of marginal reductions in costs equal the value of marginal reductions in benefits.

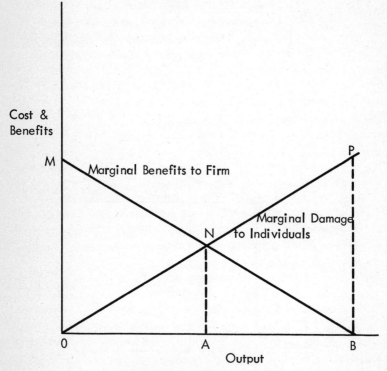

Figure 6-3. Optimum Externality

It is important to recognize that complete elimination of air pollution is not likely to be efficient. If *MB* in Figure 6-3 represented the net benefits of production after the most efficient in-plant control equipment was in use and *OP* represented damages from air pollution, legislation of a zero pollution level, output 0, would lead to a loss of benefits of *OMNA* and a net reduction in damages of *ONA* over the efficient control level.

Since the loss of benefits exceeds the reduction in damages by *OMN*, complete elimination of pollution would cost more than it was worth.

Achieving Efficient Air Quality

In the above example, it was easy to conceptualize the optimal level of air pollution control. However, the three most important problems were neglected: first, the identification of the value of damages borne by recipients of polluted air (*OP* in Figure 6-3) which is equal to the effective demand for clean air; second, determining the least-cost method of reducing effluents at any source of pollution; and, third, the mechanism by which the optimum level of control results from interaction between the polluter and the affected individuals. If an Omniscient Benevolent Despot could be put in charge of pollution control, the appropriate level of production and proper equipment for in-plant emission reduction could be dictated to the firm; as long as the polity and economy are run by human beings, a closer look at the problem is needed.

The identification of demand for clean air is a typical latent-group/public-goods problem. If members of the group had to bear the cost of clean air, a "let George do it" attitude could be expected to prevail, since each individual would benefit if the air were cleansed through the sacrifices of others. On the other hand, if costs of clean air are to be borne by producers of effluent, each individual could clamor for a zero pollution level, knowing that the costs would not fall directly on him. In either case, it is very difficult to identify the true value individuals place on clean air: this would be revealed if resources were sacrificed in direct proportion to their demands.

Generally, citizens will organize and act when air pollution becomes so severe that some individual or a small number of individuals are motivated. In this case, the public good, clean air, is demanded by a privileged or intermediate, rather than a latent, group. In addition, a political entrepreneur may realize that by initiating action on behalf of the citizens, he will realize a private payoff in the form of their support during the next election. Mobilization of one form or another is most likely to occur after a crisis situation—for example, following a period of abnormally heavy air pollution. Once air pollution is recognized as a problem with an effective demand for a solution, several alternatives are open to political entrepreneurs or leaders of groups who demand cleaner air. These alternatives include direct bargaining with polluters, recourse to the courts, and attempts to prevent air pollution by city, county, state or national legislation.[18]

In the past, litigation in the courts to prevent the use of an airshed for disposal purposes under "nuisance law" provisions has been used to limit pollution, but cases where the polluter has been held to possess a right to pollute, with air pollution being viewed as a "cost of progress," are on record.[19] It is also extremely difficult to identify and value specific damages from a single emission source, and the identification of sources of damages has become even more difficult as air pollution has become relatively worse. This is because pollution has shifted from primary pollutants (dust, smoke, etc.) to secondary pollutants (which result from photochemical or physiochemical reactions among pollutants from a variety of sources after they are in the air). Smog, for example, is not put into the air, but is the result of sunlight irradiating unburned fuels in stagnant air. Because of the number of people involved and the difficulty of valuing damages, recourse to the courts is likely to be both time-consuming and expensive, and is unlikely to lead to satisfactory solutions to pollution control.

When one moves beyond the adversary proceedings of the courtroom which, even though costly, tend to result in the revelation of damages, costs of control, and ultimately determine a level of air pollution control, it is difficult to design a system that solves all three problems simultaneously. For example, if one puts all responsibility for air pollution on the polluter, he will have the responsibility and a direct incentive to discover the least cost in-plant techniques for emission reduction. However, individuals who bear no costs related to their demands for clean air may overstate their demands—that is, they may state that they wish a higher level of pollution control than they would be willing to pay for. On the other hand, if costs of pollution control were borne by individuals demanding clean air, perhaps by paying subsidies to polluters to bribe them to reduce pollution emissions, the polluters would not have the incentive to seek the lowest cost methods of in-plant emission control.

[18] For discussions of these alternatives, see *Law and Contemporary Problems*, XXXIII (Spring 1968).

[19] *Bove v. Donner-Hanna Coke Corp.*, 142 Misc. 329, 254 N.Y.S. 403 (1931). Cited in Lawrence W. Pollack, "Legal Boundaries of Air Pollution Control—State and Local Legislative Purpose and Techniques," *Law and Contemporary Problems*, XXXIII (Spring 1968), 333–334.

Thus, the level of pollution might be higher than is optimal. Some mechanism that would require individuals demanding clean air to reveal their true preferences, provide incentives for polluters to seek least-cost methods of control, and, finally, balance the benefits of using air to dispose of pollutants against the damages of air pollution is needed.

The most common method of regulating air pollution is to create an independent agency or special district—either at the county, multi-county, or state level. The agency is usually quasijudicial and holds hearings as well as possesses a technical staff to monitor emissions, air quality and evidence brought before it in quasijudicial adversary proceedings. It is the responsibility of the agency to weigh the evidence on emissions and damages and to determine a method for reconciling demands for clean air with demands for the use of air for waste disposal, to set standards or other mechanisms for achieving desired air quality, and to enforce air pollution control regulations. Presently, a common method of control is to set standards of emissions for various pollutants and permit exceptions by special permits for polluters who would have especially high costs in meeting the standards. Standards for emissions, however, are only one way of regulating air quality. It is useful here to examine the incentives generated by setting standards along with the economist's most popular recommendations for air quality control—effluent charges or the creation of a market for "rights to pollute." [20]

Standards. Regulation by emission standards puts responsibility on the regulatory agency for determining air pollution damages, judging the alternative in-plant control techniques for feasibility, and determining a compromise air quality. After standards are set, adjustments will probably be necessary over time to take into account changes in demands for clean air, changes in the relationship between particular effluent standards and air quality, and changes in technology for in-plant emission control. One problem with standards is that there is no incentive for polluters to reduce pollution below standards or to undertake research and development to achieve lower pollution levels in the future, unless they know that future standards will be stricter than present standards. Standards do resemble a price system in that failure to meet

[20] For a discussion of these alternatives with regard to water pollution, see Allen V. Kneese and Blair T. Bower, *Managing Water Quality: Economics, Technology, Institutions* (Baltimore: Johns Hopkins Press, 1968), chs. 5–9.

standards is likely to result in a fine. A firm that calculates the fine as less expensive than meeting standards may choose to pollute and pay the fine. This would result in optimal levels of air pollution control only if the fine were equal to the damages caused by pollution; hence, the fine becomes synonymous with an effluent charge.

Effluent Charges. An alternative to setting effluent discharge standards is to levy a charge on polluters equal to the damage their pollution causes. If the charge were accurately set, the firm would then adjust output to that point where total marginal costs equaled marginal benefits (point *H,* with output *A* in Figure 6-2) and optimal output would be achieved. The difficulties for the pollution control agency with effluent charges are less severe than with the setting of standards. The agency must identify the damages from air pollution (and individuals may "overstate" their demands), but once damages are identified and charges set, firms have the incentive to compare in-plant techniques for effluent reduction and choose the least-cost method of dealing with pollution. Firms have the incentive to lower emissions to zero to reduce charges and to invest in research and development to reduce emissions and avoid charges in the future. Effluent charges could be adjusted to achieve any desired level of control, while leaving much of the technical decision-making to the polluting firms.

Rights to Pollute. An alternative to either standards or effluent charges would be the creation of a market in "rights to pollute." The air pollution control agency could issue or sell "rights" to firms to emit effluents into the air, with the total amount of permissible emissions equal to what is determined to yield a desired air quality. Because the initial distribution and number of rights are not as important as the fact that they are created to be bought and sold, a variety of initial distribution mechanisms could be used. Once rights to pollute exist, the cost of obtaining them would be permitted to fluctuate in relation to supply and demand. Firms faced with a decision of whether or not to pollute would compare the price of a right with costs of in-plant effluent reduction and select the least costly alternative. This would serve to allocate existing rights to firms for which effluent control was most costly, and firms that could introduce control at a cost lower than the market price for rights to pollute would sell their rights to firms who were willing to pay the market price. This would permit an efficient adjustment among firms to achieve desirable air quality levels without concern of the air pollution control board.

A second desirable feature of rights to pollute is that if citizens in the area should demand higher air quality, the air pollution control board could levy taxes on individuals and purchase rights to pollute from firms and retire them. This would force individuals demanding clean air to reveal their preferences by giving up resources (taxes) as they do for any public good provided by a public agency. Permitting those who demand clean air to buy up pollution rights would automatically solve the two most difficult problems in determining efficient air quality levels: it would identify the "damage" function by the amount individuals were willing to pay for clean air, and it would determine air quality levels by the selling and buying (and retirement) of pollution rights. The only enforcement required by the air pollution control agency would be to monitor emissions to guarantee compliance and to levy fines that were higher than the cost of buying rights to pollute for violations. A market for rights to pollute would set up a self-adjusting efficient level of air quality and minimize the number and difficulty of independent decisions to be exercised by a regulatory agency.

Of the three methods for air quality regulation discussed here (standards, effluent charges, and rights to pollute), the setting up of a market in rights to pollute would be expected to achieve the most efficient level of air quality: equally important, a quality level that would automatically adjust over time to take into account changes in demands for clean air or in technology for effluent reduction would be initiated. It would also force those who demand clean air to bear some of the costs—thus, the right to pollute probably would not be popular with environmental interest groups or the average citizen (even though less efficient air quality regulation would impose higher costs on consumers in general). Effluent charges would serve to encourage technological change and an efficient air quality level, but the difficulty of independently identifying the damage function remains. If a standard is imposed, the difficulty of identifying damages, independently evaluating in-plant control technology and determining an air quality level remains, and no mechanism is provided for encouraging improvements in control beyond standard requirements. Of the three techniques, the use of standards is probably inferior to either effluent charges or a market for rights to pollute, and a market for rights to pollute is superior to effluent charges for achieving an efficient level of air quality.

Extensive air quality regulation is relatively new, so it is unlikely that the evolution of institutional mechanisms in the United States for air pollution control is complete. However, an examination of a case of state and local air pollution regulation will illustrate how, over time, area-wide controls were established in one problem area and provide a background for examining the control agencies emerging since the national government has taken an increased interest in environmental control.

The Case of Los Angeles County and California

Los Angeles County was one of several areas with severe air pollution problems after World War II. In 1945, both the County and the City of Los Angeles enacted air pollution control measures and encouraged other municipalities to do the same.[21] There were some holdouts, however, and the voluntary agreement approach was not successful in obtaining county-wide regulation.

In 1947, Los Angeles County and leaders from southern California encouraged the California State Legislature to pass an enabling act authorizing counties to establish air pollution control authorities holding jurisdiction within incorporated as well as unincorporated areas to enable a county-wide approach to air pollution problems. Such enabling legislation was passed in the 1947 Air Pollution Control Act. Immediately, the Los Angeles County Board of Supervisors established an Air Pollution Control District empowered, under the Act, to levy fines and to exercise broad enforcement authority, including the establishment of emergency powers under "smog alerts." Under such conditions, the Control District officers are authorized to shut down industrial polluters or force them to shift to lower-emission fuels.

While the single-county approach was adequate for Los Angeles, it was not satisfactory for all areas in the state. In 1949, the State Legislature broadened the enabling legislation to provide for multicounty Air Pollution Control Districts that have since been used by regions such as the San Francisco Bay Area.

The establishment of Air Pollution Control Districts within the

[21] See discussion in Kenneth G. Bueche and Morris J. Schur, *Air Pollution Control—Selected Governmental Approaches: Possibilities for Colorado* (Boulder: Bureau of Governmental Research and Service, University of Colorado, 1963), ch. ii, pp. 11–14.

state did not resolve the problem of the automobile. Although the automobile had caused only a small proportion of the initial air pollution, the combination of decreased air pollution from other sources and an increase in the number of automobiles resulted in a situation where they were now directly responsible for most of the air pollution. Because of special problems related to mobility and the difficulties of identifying individual sources of pollution, the question of automobile exhaust emissions could not feasibly be dealt with by any of the local air pollution control districts.

The state was encouraged to deal with the problem on a state-wide basis; and, in 1959, the legislature passed laws (1) authorizing the State Board of Public Health to set forth standards on air quality and motor vehicle emissions and (2) establishing a Motor Vehicle Pollution Control Board with authority to certify devices for reducing automobile air pollution. The state also passed legislation to the effect that within one year after the Motor Vehicle Pollution Control Board had certified two emission-control devices, all new cars registered in the state must be equipped with them. A schedule was also set up to prescribe installation of pollution control devices on used automobiles.

The jump from county and multicounty air pollution control districts to the state level for automobile pollution control regulation appeared necessary, given the mobility of automobiles; but state-wide requirements also imposed unnecessary costs of installing pollution-control devices on cars in rural counties where they are simply unnecessary. Later, national requirements for emission control devices on automobiles superseded California regulation, but the national regulations have the same basic defect: that of imposing unnecessary costs on individuals who reside in areas where pollution is not a problem. Both California and national regulation would be more efficient if it permitted exceptions. California could exempt some rural counties and national legislation could exempt some states. This would reduce the costs for individuals in areas where, essentially, no benefits are derived from automobile emission controls.

Air pollution control in California and in Los Angeles County has been established as an important governmental function, and California presently accounts for a large proportion of all governmental expenditure on air pollution control in the United States. Primarily, regulation is effected by setting effluent standards, some of which are adjusted depending on air quality at a particular time. For example, during times of severe air pollution, firms can be required to change to lower-emission fuels or shut down. Violators of emission standards are fined. There is insufficient evidence to evaluate the overall efficiency with which present emission standards meet individual demands for clean air, encourage technological change by polluting firms to reduce effluents, and ultimately arrive at an optimal level of air pollution control. It is likely that improvements have been made over the "no control" situation or reliance completely on suits brought in the courts for damages by individual polluters, but the magnitude of present improvements and the potential for further improvements will remain unknown until additional research is completed.

Recent National Development

Recent legislation at the federal level has increasingly rationalized the regulation of air pollution. The basic strategy appears to be to finance, and often conduct, research into effects of air pollution at the national level, because the research is too expensive to be undertaken by any smaller political unit and once the research is complete, it becomes available like a public good to anyone who wants to use it. With a few exceptions, however, the national government is not attempting to develop regulations on air pollution; instead, it relies on the states and their subunits to determine airshed boundaries and methods of regulation for pollution within those sheds. There has been explicit recognition that since not every airshed has equal assimilative capacity, different regulations are needed in different places, and industrial location choice should be definitely influenced by air pollution considerations and determined by the specific assimilative capacity of any given airshed for waste disposal.[22]

The national government also provides subsidies, as do several state governments, for firms adopting ar pollution control techniques. This is because many firms could make somewhat legitimate claims to use of the airshed for waste disposal, even though all of the firms put together had the potential for making the atmosphere unbreathable. Subsidies therefore offer one way in which beneficiaries of the public good—

[22] See Harold W. Kennedy and Martin E. Weekes, "Control of Automobile Emissions—California Experience and the Federal Legislation," and Robert Martin and Lloyd Symington, "A Guide to the Air Quality Act of 1967," *Law and Contemporary Problems*, XXXIII (Spring 1968), 251, 256.

citizens breathing clean air—contribute to paying for that good, but subsidies on a local, rather than national, level would relate benefits to costs more closely.

At the present time, the national government and most state governments still rely on effluent standards combined with fines and subsidies determined by a mixture of voting on legislation and bargaining among the parties involved in regulating air pollution and the potential polluters.[23] Hopefully, experimentation with effluent charges and rights to pollute will take place along with improved research on all aspects of air pollution control to achieve an efficient institutional structure for dealing with a problem that is likely to be increasingly important over time.

Conclusions on Air Pollution Control

The theoretical constructs developed in Chapters 1 to 3 appear appropriate for an examination of air pollution and the development of institutional mechanisms for its control. Air pollution possesses characteristics of externalities and public goods; it requires collective action; and its boundaries may differ from those of other political units. The evolution of institutional arrangements is not complete, and there is insufficient evidence for a rigorous evaluation of the present state of institutional development. Developments so far, however, resemble those one would predict from a model based on economic approaches to the study of the public sector.

CONCLUSIONS

The areas of education and air pollution control are but two of many examples that could be selected for examination in the theoretical framework provided in Chapters 1 through 3. While both of the analyses are relatively brief, they do appear to grasp the essential problems in both areas and to help in explaining the outcomes of the political processes.

The examination of education indicated that efficient institutional arrangements do not appear to exist in the largest school systems for

---

[23] George Hagevik, "Legislating for Air Quality Management: Reducing Theory to Practice," *Law and Contemporary Problems*, XXXIII (Spring 1968), 369–398.

meeting individual demands while taking into account spillovers and equalization objectives; the analysis does provide a basis for normative judgment if one accepts the individualistic framework of this analysis. The present systems are explainable, however, in light of the historical development of monopoly school systems and predicted attempts by professionals in any area to be primarily concerned with their own interests and their interpretations of the interests of their clients. Given the flexibility in the American system, I would predict, however, that increasing recognition of the divergencies between objectives of professionals in the big-city school systems and citizen demands will eventually lead to diminished authority by the professional organizations and more efficient institutional arrangements for meeting demands for education in the big-city systems.

The examination of air pollution regulation illustrates a classic case where outputs of the public policy process appear to be evolving toward conditions for efficient arrangements stipulated by the model. The interesting question over time, however, is whether institutional development will continue or whether rigidity will set in and preclude modifications to adjust to a changing situation.

This examination of two functional areas illustrates the applicability of the conceptual framework used. Hopefully, it will stimulate an in-depth study of these and other functional areas, thereby increasing an understanding of the structure and functioning of the American public economy.

Chapter 7

FISCAL DIVERSITY AND INCOME
REDISTRIBUTION IN A FEDERAL SYSTEM

INTRODUCTION

The issues related to diverse fiscal resources among governmental units in metropolitan areas and policies for income redistribution among individuals within and between political units in a federal system present interesting problems for analysis within the framework developed in this study. This is especially the case because the questions of fiscal diversity and income redistribution were passed over in the analysis of metropolitan area governmental organization and education, and because questions of income distribution are seldom treated within individualistic "benefits received" taxation models.

A summary of trends in the location of economic activities in metropolitan areas that produce fiscal diversity among local government units introduces this chapter. An analysis of fiscal diversity and income redistribution policies in a federal system will follow.

TRENDS IN METROPOLITAN AREAS

Decentralization

Trends in the location of economic activities in metropolitan areas are well established empirically and within the theoretical frameworks of economics and geography. The trends have existed at least since the introduction of the truck and automobile early in the 20th century. There is little evidence that they will be reversed during this century.[1]

[1] For examples, see John R. Meyer, John F. Kain, and Martin Wohl, *The Urban Transportation Problem* (Cambridge, Mass.: Harvard University

Decentralization—the movement of economic activity from the center of a metropolitan area to outlying areas—is the major trend of relocation. The first shift is usually toward residential relocation because it is relatively cheaper to construct new housing on vacant land in the suburbs and travel to work in the central city[2] than to demolish old housing and rebuild in the central city itself. Retail firms follow residents to the suburbs. Because of the exodus, retail sales have decreased in many central cities. For example, between 1958 and 1963, retail sales decreased in twenty-eight central business districts and eleven central cities of the thirty-seven largest Standard Metropolitan Statistical Areas (SMSA) in the United States. Twenty-one of the thirty-seven central cities also had absolute declines in manufacturing employment between 1958–63, continuing the trend of new manufacturing activities to locate on large tracts of suburban land rather than squeeze into the older manufacturing areas of central cities. The other major economic activities, wholesaling and services, have not absolutely declined in most central cities, but have been growing more slowly in the central cities than in the surrounding urban areas.[3]

In addition to declines in economic activity in central cities, the central cities are also experiencing significant shifts in the socioeconomic characteristics of their resident populations. A selective migration process is resulting in low-income families, and often racial minorities, being concentrated within the older central city while middle- and high-income families have moved to suburban areas. At the same time, many central cities have lost in total population. The result is a decline from 65 percent of SMSA population in central cities in 1920 to 50 percent in 1962, and

---

Press, 1965), chs. 2, 3; Hugh O. Nourse, *Regional Economics* (New York: McGraw-Hill, 1968), chs. 2, 3, 4, & 5; William Alonso, *Location and Land Use* (Cambridge, Mass.: Harvard University Press, 1964); and Leon Moses and Harold F. Williamson, Jr., "The Location of Economic Activity in Cities," *American Economic Review,* LVII (May 1967), 211–222.

[2] The central city is the largest city in a metropolitan area. The central business district is the traditional downtown business area of the central city. A Standard Metropolitan Statistical Areas (SMSA), also referred to as an urban area, is a county or group of contiguous counties that contains at least one city of 50,000 inhabitants or more. Suburbs are the areas within the SMSA outside the central city.

[3] Advisory Commission on Intergovernmental Relations, *Fiscal Balance in the American Federal System,* Vol. 2, *Metropolitan Fiscal Disparities* (Washington, D.C.: U.S. Government Printing Office, 1967), pp. 50–54.

an expected 40 percent by 1975, with larger percentage declines in larger SMSAs.[4]

Changes in the location of economic activities and shifts in population have noticeable effects on the fiscal situation of central cities and surrounding areas. In general, central cities are left with a population group that "demands" relatively large expenditures in the public sector, while fiscal resources are declining. Concurrently, many middle- and high-income families who formerly paid high taxes because their suburban areas lacked an industrial or business activity tax base are finding that their tax load has been decreased in proportion to an increase in business activity. Thus, central cities are increasingly in fiscal trouble, while suburban areas are increasingly better able to finance higher levels of public goods and services.

Diversification

To discuss changes in metropolitan areas in a central city/suburban dichotomy, however, conceals much of what has been happening in metropolitan areas. The suburbs are not homogeneous, sprawling areas of upper middle-class residence. They are, in fact, as diverse as central cities. While older central cities have been decentralized, smaller concentrations of homogeneous economic activities have begun in other parts of urbanized areas. Families with similar tastes locate together, and often, incorporate as a municipality to preserve their selective residential environment. Retailers group together in shopping centers serving many neighboring residential areas, often in a rather small municipality whose residents benefit from the large amount of economic activity and corresponding tax base the retailers possess. Other areas, particularly large areas of flat land where rail or water transportation is good, become centers for manufacturing, with employees commuting from adjacent residential areas. The results are often similar to those indicated in the study of the Los Angeles metropolitan area: diverse population concentrations and land uses, requiring quite different public goods and services from their respective governmental units. Areas are incorporated that are not balanced agglomerations of residences, retailing, wholesaling, manufacturing and offices, as cities were in the nineteenth century; they are specialized, with one function or another predominating.

As with Los Angeles County, this specialization can be expected to

[4] *Ibid.,* p. 30.

result in very diverse levels and mixes of public goods and services demanded by citizens in the various political units; thus, comparisons of
their relative efficiency in meeting individual demands may be extremely difficult. If state enabling legislation is flexible, however, as in
California, there are reasons to expect that local public officials will
respond to meeting the demands of their constituents quite efficiently, at
least where extensive spillovers of costs and benefits to other jurisdictions
are not involved.

Population and economic diversity within local political units produce different capabilities for financing public goods and services. This
fiscal diversity may or may not create a problem of efficiently allocating
resources in the public sector to meet effective demands, but for a
variety of reasons, fiscal diversity has traditionally been described as a
problem.[5] Among these reasons are that poor areas do not have resources
to finance "needed" public services, and wealthy areas escape their "fair
share" of taxation because they do not have to support lower-income areas
in the metropolitan region. Another allegation is that declining central
cities are being "exploited" by suburban commuters who use city streets
and facilities but pay their property taxes to jurisdictions outside the city.
It is useful to examine these in order to indicate which are economic
inefficiencies in the allocation of resources rather than deliberate attempts
to shift the burden of taxation to others. The use of the individualistic
model for analyzing income distribution problems will also identify some
significant policy constraints in the American public economy.

DEALING WITH FISCAL DIVERSITY

Spillovers

Fiscal diversity leads to allocational efficiency problems when a local
governmental unit generates negative spillovers to individuals in adjacent areas where—perhaps because of low income—provision for a

---

[5] ACIR, *Fiscal Balance in the American Federal System,* Vol. I (Washington, D.C.: U.S. Government Printing Office, 1967), pp. xxii, 2, 5, 20;
ACIR, *Fiscal Balance,* Vol. II, pp. 1–3; ACIR, *Metropolitan Social and Economic Disparities* (Washington, D.C.: U.S. Government Printing Office, 1965),
p. 5; Committee for Economic Development, *Reshaping Government in
Metropolitan Areas* (New York: Committee for Economic Development,
February, 1970).

particular public good or service is low. For example, failing to eradicate mosquito-breeding areas, maintaining open garbage dumps, permitting untreated sewage to enter rivers or lakes, or failing to provide adequate schooling for local children may generate negative spillovers to adjacent jurisdictions. Where individuals in the local unit with low public-sector services have inadequate incomes to remove the negative externalities, even if compliance is legally required by a higher level of government, external resources must be provided if the spillover is to be removed. Spillovers of this type are generally handled by providing conditional financial aid from a larger, more inclusive governmental unit, so that tax revenues are collected over a larger area to finance those functions that benefit areas wider than the jurisdiction producing the good or service. Both the state and the federal government have numerous grant programs with equalization clauses for these purposes.[6]

A second method of resolving small unit spillover problems is to shift the functions of demand, financing, and provision of the good to a more inclusive governmental unit. This was the pattern taken in dealing with most air pollution control problems discussed in the last chapter; it is often the pattern used in other environmental management areas, such as water quality management or solid waste disposal.[7]

A slightly different type of spillover problem is the alleged exploitation of central cities by suburban commuters who work in the central city, use city streets, police, and other city services, but pay their property taxes to the local government of their place of residence. There is a positive correlation between the proportion of population in a metropolitan area residing outside of the central city and the governmental per capita expenditures within the central city, which may indicate that large suburban populations increase central-city fiscal requirements.[8] How-

[6] Selma J. Mushkin and John F. Cotton, *Sharing Federal Funds for State and Local Needs* (New York: Praeger, 1969), ch. 3; ACIR, *Fiscal Balance*, Vol. I, pp. 140–149; ACIR, *The Role of Equalization in Federal Grants* (Washington, D.C.: U.S. Government Printing Office, 1964).

[7] Allen V. Kneese and Blair T. Bower, *Managing Water Quality: Economics, Technology, Institutions* (Baltimore: Johns Hopkins Press, 1968), ch. 13; Lewis C. Green, "State Control of Interstate Air Pollution," *Law and Contemporary Problems*, XXXIII (Spring, 1968), 320–325.

[8] ACIR, *Fiscal Balance*, Vol. II, pp. 35, 76, 103–110; David Davies, "Financing Urban Functions and Services," *Law and Contemporary Problems*, XXX (Winter 1965), 138; Amos H. Hawley, "Metropolitan Population

ever, suburbanities also transact considerable business in central cities and some proportion of property and business tax revenue must be attributed to commuters who raise the level of economic activity and, hence, land values in the central city.[9] Thus, it cannot be said a priori that suburbanites generate either net costs or net benefits to central cities. It is, in fact, quite likely that most central cities would be in a less favorable fiscal position if commuters found employment outside the city and carried on virtually all their economic activities outside its boundaries. This could occur if central cities should attempt to tax nonresidents for an amount greater than the net gain the nonresidents derive from being employed or doing business in the city.

Income Redistribution in a Federal System

Many of the criticisms of fiscal diversity in metropolitan areas arise not from obvious cases of spillovers, but from concern with income distribution. Individuals in poorer political units are simply "judged" to have too low a level of particular public goods and services, and it is suggested that wealthier areas should finance a higher level of public goods for poor areas. While income redistribution questions usually are examined outside the framework of an individualistic benefits-received taxation model[10] and philosophical debates on income distribution issues range far and wide,[11] it is possible to treat income redistribution within the model developed in this book.[12] The conclusions may not satisfy those who have high demands for income redistribution and wish to

and Municipal Government Expenditures in Central Cities," *Journal of Social Issues,* VII (Nos. 1 & 2, 1951), 100–108; Harvey E. Brazer, *City Expenditures in the United States* (New York: National Bureau of Economic Research, 1959), pp. 54–59.

[9] For example, Hirsch estimated that in Clayton, Missouri, 48.43% of the real property tax was borne by nonresidents. Werner Z. Hirsch, Elbert W. Segelhorst, and Morton J. Marcus, *Spill-over of Public Education Costs and Benefits* (Los Angeles: University of California, Institute of Government and Public Affairs, 1964), p. 82.

[10] Usually taxation is divided into benefits-received and ability-to-pay criteria. See Harold M. Groves, *Financing Government* (New York: Holt, Rinehart & Winston, 1964), ch. 2.

[11] For a good selection, see Edward C. Budd, ed., *Inequality and Poverty* (New York: Norton, 1967).

[12] For a similar approach, see Edgar O. Olsen, "A Normative Theory of Transfers," *Public Choice,* VI (Spring 1969), 39–58.

impose their own social welfare function, but they do go a long way toward indicating the rationale behind the limited income redistribution that takes place within and between local government units in metropolitan areas.

In the individualistic model, a state of income distribution different from the one determined by current institutions is viewed as an economic good for which there must be an effective demand. Thus, an individual's demand for income redistribution would be treated as a demand for a public good: in this case, a particular state of resources-claim distribution which, when achieved, is consumed by everyone, with the effective demand being the amount of resources or price one is willing to pay for achieving a particular income distribution. The demands of low-income individuals for an increased share of resources without any sacrifice are regarded as noneconomic or noneffective demands (like any "demand" of something for nothing), and satisfaction of these demands does not increase economic efficiency in its broadest sense. Demands of this type, if imposed on other individuals, are political externalities imposed through the political process on the individuals from whom resources are taken.

It is important to remember that income redistribution, or programs with redistributional consequences, are not excluded from the model based on individual preferences; rather, they may be interpreted as resulting from the effective articulation of demands based on altruism, consumption externalities, any other motivation strong enough to result in the sacrifice of resources, as well as the imposition of political externalities in an exploitative manner. Many high-income individuals act as if they benefit from raising the consumption of low-income families, or bear reduced externally-imposed costs by paying for increased consumption of particular goods by low-income families.[13] Thus, a priori, some (but not the exact amount) income redistribution in an individualistic society can be predicted.

Much of the analysis of income diversity among governmental units has focused on single metropolitan areas, implying that the metropolitan area is an appropriate unit for undertaking income redistribution programs.[14] However, most metropolitan areas lack an appropriately sized governmental unit for this purpose. Other subnational political units,

---

[13] For example, see James Q. Wilson and Edward C. Banfield, "Public-Regardingness as a Value Premise in Voting Behavior," *American Political Science Review*, LVIII (December 1964), 876–887.

[14] ACIR, *Fiscal Balance*, Vol. II.

including municipalities, counties and states, do not appear to undertake as much income redistribution as the federal government. Studies of
tax and expenditure incidence indicate that taxes are more regressive at
state and local levels and that the overall tax/expenditure impact is more
redistributional to low-income families at the federal level.[15] For example, the Tax Foundation estimates that families in the lowest income
class (under $2,000) received federal benefits of six times their federal
tax share and state and local benefits 2.3 times their state and local
taxes. A similar comparison of high-income families (over $15,000) indi-
cated federal benefits of three-tenths of the tax burden and state and
local benefits of six-tenths of the tax burden.[16]

Two elements in the studies make their results appear more redistributive than they actually are: one is the use of expenditure to measure
benefit, the other the use of per-family allocation of general expenditures.
The use of expenditures to measure benefits implies that governmental
expenditure programs are valued by the recipients at an amount equal to
the total cost of the program. This is very unlikely; for example, it is
estimated that $109 per unit must be expended to produce a public hous-
ing unit with a market value of $75.[17] Thus, to estimate benefits to
families from program expenditures is to overstate their value to low-
income families—possibly by large amounts. The division of general
expenditures on a per-family basis (or allocation of one-half of general
expenditures on this basis in the Tax Foundation study) is based on the
assumption that benefits are distributed equally. In fact, the measure of
benefits to an individual is the amount he is willing to pay for them,
and it is very likely that high-income families place higher values on
most general governmental expenditures than do low-income families.

Because subnational units do not engage as extensively in income
redistribution programs as the federal government, it may be that there
is either less effective demand at the subnational level or some characteristics of the redistribution process per se that prevent its use by small

[15] For examples, see Tax Foundation, *Tax Burdens and Benefits of Government Expenditures by Income Class, 1961 and 1965* (New York: Tax
Foundation, 1967); W. Irwin Gillespie, "Effects of Public Expenditures on
the Distribution of Income," in Richard A. Musgrave, ed., *Essays in Fiscal
Federalism* (Washington, D.C.: Brookings, 1965), pp. 122–186.

[16] Tax Foundation, *Tax Burdens and Benefits*, p. 32.

[17] Robert L. Bish, "Public Housing: The Magnitude and Distribution
of Direct Benefits and Effects on Housing Consumption," *Journal of Regional Science,* IX (December 1969), 430, 437.

governmental units. If either of these situations exist, the creation of a metropolitan-wide unit for income redistributive purposes would not be expected to lead to higher levels of redistribution than presently observed.

From casual observation, one would expect a *greater* effective demand for income redistribution on local rather than national levels. After all, higher consumption externalities may accrue from raising the incomes of low-income families who are near enough to be observed, and any reduced negative spillovers are likely to accrue from transfers to local, rather than distant, families. If this is the case, it is likely that something in the nature of the income redistribution process per se in the American public economy limits its use by smaller political units, and it would be useful to examine the process more closely to see why.

If states of income distribution different from the existing distribution are treated as public goods for which there must be an effective demand, one would expect the amount of redistribution demanded to decrease, with an increase in price for those making net contributions to the process. Thus, if a local political unit started a redistribution program in response to demands by its higher-income citizens, some equilibrium level of redistribution could be expected. This equilibrium, however, is unlikely to be stable. If a single small political unit carried out income redistribution by transferring either goods or cash to the poor within its boundaries, poor individuals residing elsewhere would have an incentive to migrate into the redistributing unit. With each immigrant, the price of any particular level of redistribution would rise, and less redistribution would result per family. Some high-income families would also feel that the price for the redistribution achieved was too high and migrate to a unit with a lower level of redistribution, perhaps composed almost exclusively of individuals with relatively high incomes requiring no redistributive policies or one with a regressive tax structure. After all, any single high-income individual could move out of the unit, and make net gains, without substantially reducing the redistribution in the unit he left; thus, he could obtain public good consumption externalities from knowing that the low-income families in the unit still received redistributive program benefits. However, the net effects of many low-income immigrants and many high-income emigrants would be to reduce the effective demand for income redistribution and raise the price of the redistribution, so that the amount of redistribution would be predicted to decrease until individuals had nothing to gain by migration—a level that may be quite low.

The extent to which the dual migration would occur depends not only on fiscal advantage, but on the residential and employment alternatives elsewhere and the distance that must be moved. Within a single metropolitan area, it is often quite feasible to move one's residence and, hence, major taxpaying location, without changing employment location; thus, independent governmental units within a metropolitan area may face extremely severe constraints on income redistributive policies, including the use of progressive taxation for general governmental expenditures. As distance between units requires longer migrations, a greater degree of redistribution may be feasible, although many individuals feel that states are not large enough—especially in the East—to undertake extensive redistribution without running into the dual migration problem. Perhaps only an entire country can pursue extensive income redistribution, and then, only because restriction of low-income immigrants from abroad is possible.

In general, because of the lack of migration constraints, income redistribution to low-income families in a federal system, if there is an effective demand for it, will be feasible only in higher levels of governmental units. Even if an effective demand exists on the local level, it is unlikely that subnational governmental units will ever embark on redistributive programs of their own. Extensive local redistributive programs will either have to be financed by the federal government or undertaken simultaneously by a relatively large governmental unit such as a state government. While a metropolitan-wide unit could undertake relatively more redistribution than individual municipalities, in most cases, it would not have greater capabilities than existing states; thus, its creation would not necessarily resolve the fiscal diversity problem in metropolitan areas. If fiscal diversity is going to be ended, it must be dealt with on state or national levels, and policy at a national level will become imperative in the future as a larger number of firms and individuals are free to migrate across the entire country seeking desirable residential and business situations.

Geographically Based Programs

If national programs for income distribution are going to be developed—many of the grant programs do already contain equalizing formulae—two approaches can be used: one would focus on political units, as analysts of fiscal diversity have done, and create grant programs to help those units with low-income populations finance greater public sector activity with federal funds; the other would focus on low-income individuals and provide them with supplementary income, which they could then spend in either the public or private sector. Much of the focus in metropolitan areas has been on political units or geographically based redistribution. Model Cities is a good example, where the focus is on residents in a particular area, rather than on low-income individuals per se.

Geographically based programs, however, appear to have some severe potential disadvantages in a changing economy, especially when most of them are focused on low-income populations residing in obsolete areas of central cities where economic activity and employment opportunities are declining and the cost of starting new businesses is very high. It appears undesirable to concentrate benefits for low-income individuals in central cities—and encourage immigration to obsolete areas and discourage emigration from the aging core city—when new job opportunities are increasingly dispersed elsewhere in the metropolitan area.[18] Perhaps geographically based central-city programs will provide some short-term benefit but, being in opposition to the more efficient dispersal patterns emerging in metropolitan areas, it is likely that they will be costly.[19] And the higher the cost, the lower the level of redistribution that one would expect to occur.

Two alternatives to geographically based core city programs are national income redistribution with a guaranteed annual income or negative income tax to assist low-income families wherever they locate,[20] and geographically based programs that focus on areas with a potential

[18] Many Economic Development Districts, the political units created to raise low incomes in rural areas, were originally too small to sustain economic growth. The recent focus, however, is on relatively large EDDs containing a "growth pole" to which individuals can migrate to seek improved employment opportunities and higher incomes. The larger district avoids the problem of trying to generate economic growth in an area where sustaining it would require continual external subsidies.

[19] Bernard H. Booms and James E. Ward, Jr., "The Cons of Black Capitalism," *Business Horizons,* VII (October 1969), 17–26; John F. Kain and Joseph J. Persky, "Alternatives to the Gilded Ghetto," *The Public Interest,* 14 (Winter 1969), 74–87; Walter W. Heller, Richard Ruggles, Lyle C. Fitch, Carl S. Shoup, and Harvey E. Brazer, *Revenue Sharing and the City* (Baltimore: Johns Hopkins Press, 1968).

[20] Christopher Green, *Negative Taxes and the Poverty Problem* (Washington, D.C.: Brookings, 1967).

for self-sustaining economic growth.[21] A graduated negative income tax would encourage low-income families to follow employment opportunities wherever they exist, without net reductions in income by making cash available everywhere rather than just in central cities. This would assist in the dispersion of low-income families from central cities and might reduce the flow of immigrants to those cities. It might also lessen problems caused by a concentration of low-income families in particular locations. The non-geographic based program would also provide assistance to low-income families who reside in political units where the average income level is too high for geographically based support programs and local public goods and services are financed by a regressive tax system.

Geographically based programs in areas where self-sustaining economic growth is likely would assist low-income families who live in, or migrate to, the growing area and provide incentives for that migration. Such programs, however, leave untouched many low-income individuals who lack mobility or for whom net benefits from migration would be quite small. Niles Hansen provides an excellent analysis of non-urban geographically based programs for dealing with rural and urban poverty simultaneously that would appear to be superior to urban-oriented income redistribution programs and would be valuable supplements to a program such as the negative income tax.[22]

CONCLUSIONS

The locations of economic activities in metropolitan areas have undergone considerable change in the twentieth century, and further change along similar lines is expected. These changes have reduced the central city, which was formerly the center of virtually all economic activity and was surrounded by farms and rural areas, to a relatively impoverished political unit, while specialized concentrations of economic activities with their own political structures have thrived in the rest of the urban area.

The diverse political units in metropolitan areas require diverse

[21] Niles M. Hansen, *Rural Poverty and the Urban Crisis: A Strategy for Regional Development* (Bloomington, Indiana: Indiana University Press, 1970).
[22] *Ibid.*

public goods and services in response to local demands, and some units are able to finance higher levels of public goods and services than others. This fiscal diversity has been viewed as a problem by many individuals. If fiscal diversity per se does result in economic problems, it appears that an effective demand for income redistribution exercised through national policies would yield the most efficient solutions. In choosing national approaches, a non-geographically based program, such as a negative income tax, perhaps supplemented with non-urban area economic growth policies, appears to be much more consistent with the trends in metropolitan areas than programs focused on core city residents; thus, it would be much more likely to succeed in its objective of raising the public and private goods consumption levels of low-income families.

Chapter 8

A NOTE ON THE POLITICAL REFORM TRADITION

INTRODUCTION

Recommendations for changes in the structure of government in metropolitan areas are continually being made by academicians, consultants, citizen groups, and others concerned with public policy problems. During the twentieth century, a tradition, referred to earlier as the "political reform tradition," has dominated reform recommendations in the United States. Because the conclusions reached here as to what institutional arrangements would facilitate an efficient and responsive public economy are so different from most political reform recommendations, an examination of political reform positions in relation to the public choice approach should assist readers in identifying the basis for these differences. Since comprehensive analyses of the political reform tradition can be found elsewhere, this analysis will be relatively brief.

THE REFORM TRADITION

Recent examples of reform literature are the Committee for Economic Development's *Modernizing Local Government* and *Reshaping Government in Metropolitan Areas*.[1] Earlier examples include Chester Maxey's

[1] Committee for Economic Development, *Modernizing Local Government* (New York: CED, 1966); *idem, Reshaping Government in Metropolitan Areas* (New York: CED, 1970).

"The Political Integration of Metropolitan Communities," in the 1922 *National Municipal Review*;[2] Paul Studenski's study for the National Municipal League in 1930, *The Government of Metropolitan Areas in the United States*;[3] Victor Jones' *Metropolitan Government* published in 1942;[4] and John Bollen's study for The Council of State Governments, *The States and the Metropolitan Problems,* published in 1956.[5] Many other examples could be cited.[6] Two well-known reform-oriented organizations are the National Municipal League and the League of Women Voters.

The reform tradition has presented a theoretical framework for analyzing problems and a set of solutions for them that are fairly consistent, even though several of the underlying assumptions are not often made explicit and very little empirical analysis has been accumulated to provide evidence for the appropriateness of the suggested solutions.[7] At risk of attributing more logical consistency to reform proposals than any one of them may contain, I will attempt to indicate the most important common positions relating to metropolitan areas (rather than to reform of a single governmental organization) and to compare them with the approach used in this study. They include contentions that the "public interest" should take precedence over individual interests; political fragmentation leads to chaos; equal service levels are desirable area-wide; the complexity of governmental structures prevents citizen control; and political units should be large enough to achieve economies of scale. Each of these elements will be analyzed in turn.

[2] Vol. XI (August, 1922), 229–253.

[3] (New York: National Municipal League, 1930).

[4] (Chicago: University of Chicago Press, 1942).

[5] (Chicago: Council of State Governments, 1956).

[6] John C. Bollens, *Special District Governments in the United States* (Berkeley and Los Angeles: University of California Press, 1957); Victor Jones, "Local Government Organization in Metropolitan Areas: Its Relation to Urban Redevelopment," in Coleman Woodbury, ed., *The Future of Cities and Urban Redevelopment* (Chicago: University of Chicago Press, 1953), 481–606; Herbert A. Simon, *Fiscal Aspects of Metropolitan Consolidation* (Berkeley: Bureau of Public Administration, University of California, 1943).

[7] Norton E. Long, "Recent Theories and Problems of Local Government," in Carl J. Friedrich and Seymour E. Harris, eds., *Public Policy,* VIII (Cambridge: Graduate School of Public Administration, Harvard University, 1958), pp. 285–295.

The Public Interest Should Take Precedence over Individual Interests

Virtually all political reform literature uses the "community" or "public" rather than the individual as the basic unit for analysis. The analytical and ethical problem, usually overlooked, is how to define the "public interest" if it exists apart from the interests of the individuals who compose the public.[8] I do not have an answer for this problem.

The achievement of any particular public interest usually results in benefits for some individuals and costs for others. It would appear that identification of benefits and costs in relation to the individuals who bear them would be more useful than the designation of programs that result in specific benefits to particular individuals as being in the "public interest." Too often, the public interest, as expressed by political reformers, coincides with policies that benefit non-minority group, middle- and upper-middle-income class individuals, to the neglect of minority preferences—and most political reformers are of the middle- and upper-income classes. One can easily conclude from an analysis of political reform recommendations that a particular socioeconomic group wishes to benevolently and paternally institute its own preferences, which it labels the "public interest," in the political system, and that it should be regarded as any other self-interested partisan rather than as "expert" on governmental organization. If this is the case, it is not surprising that political reformers recommend a single hierarchically organized area-wide metropolitan government to force small local communities to act in the public interest. Small communities, whose preferences differ from those of the reformers, resist such an imposition and attempt to maintain institutions that respond to their own interests.

Political Fragmentation Leads to Chaos

An assertion that appears to underlie all political reform recommendations is that coordination can be achieved only through hierarchical organization. Overlapping jurisdictions and duplication of functions

[8] This appears to be a common position of political reformers. See Charles R. Adrian, "Metropology: Folklore and Field Research," *Public Administration Review*, XXI (Summer, 1961), 152–153; Long, "Recent Theories," p. 289; Alan A. Altshuler, *The City Planning Process* (Ithaca, N.Y.: Cornell University Press, 1965), ch. 5; see also Anthony Downs, "The Public Interest: Its Meaning in a Democracy," *Social Research*, XXIX (Spring, 1962).

are judged ipso facto to result in uncoordinated and inefficient provision of public goods and services; thus, efficiency in the public economy would be increased if fragmentation of political authority were eliminated. In metropolitan areas, this would be brought about by the creation of a single, hierarchically organized, area-wide government to replace all existing political units.[9]

The assertion that hierarchical relationships are necessary to achieve coordination is theoretically and empirically false. The best theoretical analyses of coordination obtained through non-hierarchical mechanisms are found in economic theory of the price and market systems—and Adam Smith himself provides sufficient evidence to destroy the assumed need for hierarchical organization with regard to many activities. The theoretical foundation for non-hierarchical, or bargained, coordination in the public sector has been more recently advanced, especially in the writings of Roland McKean, Charles Lindblom, Robert Dahl, Vincent Ostrom, Robert Warren, and myself. Many of the important elements of these analyses are presented in Chapters 3 and 4.[10]

[9] Bollens, *The States and the Metropolitan Problem*, pp. 17–18; CED, *Modernizing Local Government*, pp. 11, 13; Jones, *Metropolitan Government*, pp. 23–24; Victor Jones, in Woodbury, ed., *Future of Cities*, pp. 485, 530; Chester C. Maxey, in *National Municipal Review*, p. 229.

[10] Roland N. McKean, "The Unseen Hand in Government," *American Economic Review*, LV (June, 1965), 496–506; Robert A. Dahl and Charles E. Lindblom, *Politics, Economics, and Welfare* (New York: Harper & Row, 1953); Charles E. Lindblom and David Braybrooke, *A Strategy of Decision* (New York: Free Press, 1963); Charles E. Lindblom, "Policy Analysis," *American Economic Review*, XLVIII (June, 1958), 298–312; *idem*, "Tinbergen on Policy-Making," *Journal of Political Economy*, LXVI (December, 1958), 531–538; *idem*, "The Science of 'Muddling Through,'" *Public Administration Review*, XIX (Spring, 1959), 79–88; Vincent Ostrom, "The Politics of Administration," Mimeographed. (Bloomington: Department of Government, Indiana University); *idem*, "Operational Federalism: Organization for the Provision of Public Services in the American Federal System," *Public Choice*, VI (Spring, 1969), 1–17; Vincent Ostrom, Charles M. Tiebout, and Robert O. Warren, "The Organization of Government in Metropolitan Areas: A Theoretical Inquiry," *American Political Science Review*, LV (December, 1961), 831–842; Robert O. Warren, "A Municipal Services Market Model of Metropolitan Organization," *Journal of the American Institute of Planners*, XXX (August, 1964), 193–204; *Idem*, *Government in Metropolitan Regions: A Reappraisal of Fractionated Political Organization* (Davis, California: Institute of Governmental Affairs, University of California, 1966); Robert L. Bish, "A Comment on V. P. Duggal's 'Is There an Unseen Hand in Government?'" *Annals of Public and Co-operative Economy*, XXXIX

Theoretical studies have included empirical analysis of coordination occurring without hierarchical relationships, as in Los Angeles County. Cooperative agreements and the creation of area-wide special districts achieved by bargaining have permitted area-wide approaches to problems in other metropolitan areas as well.

Once it is recognized that coordination in the public economy can be effected by non-hierarchical means, the question becomes one of the relative efficiency of hierarchical versus other organizational modes (including smaller hierarchies) to meet citizen references. If one assumes that a public interest exists apart from individual interests, and that it can be uniquely discovered by the executive and legislature of an area-wide government, a hierarchy may be the most efficient way to impose that interest on individuals and smaller communities in the area. If one assumes that individuals have different interests and that one of the major functions of political organization is to assist individuals to articulate those interests and find new solutions to problems, a closer look at political organization is necessary.

There is very little evidence to support the position that a single, hierarchically organized government would meet citizen preferences in metropolitan areas most efficiently.[11] The problems of the City of Los Angeles government in satisfying minorities in Watts was examined in Chapter 5, and the discussion of big-city education in Chapter 6 offered additional evidence on the problems of hierarchical response to minority demands. Other failures, such as breakdowns in basic services like police protection and garbage removal, are frequently reported in daily newspapers. In fact, the failure of New York City government to provide basic police services has caused its citizens to form private, voluntary police patrol organizations to provide what is usually a publicly provided service.[12] Unfortunately, at the present time, sufficient empirical data do not exist to make a firm conclusion as to the relative efficiency of hierarchical and non-hierarchical government organization

---

(January–March, 1968), 89–94; *idem,* "The American Public Economy as a Single Firm: Reply to Duggal," *Annals of Public and Co-operative Economy,* XL (July–September, 1969), 361–365.

[11] For contrary evidence, see Robert L. Lineberry and Edmund P. Fowler, "Reformism and Public Policies in American Cities," in James Q. Wilson, ed., *City Politics and Public Policy* (New York: Wiley, 1968).

[12] Vincent Ostrom, "A Political Scientist's Perspective of Government Efficiency," *The Review,* XII (Winter, 1970), 9–10.

in metropolitan areas. However, if the theoretical constructs developed in this book identify the important aspects of public sector organization, one can conclude that a single area-wide governmental unit to handle all public functions in metropolitan areas is unlikely to be as responsive or efficient in meeting citizen demands as a polycentric political structure. This is especially the case as metropolitan areas grow larger (fifteen to twenty million persons in the Northeast) and more diverse.

Equal Service Levels are Desirable Area–Wide

A common political reform criticism is that service levels are unequal in different areas of a metropolis.[13] This critique, and the corresponding assertion that equal public goods and services levels are desirable, could result from either of two alternative assumptions. One could assume that all individuals have identical tastes and incomes, and thus desire to purchase the same mix of all goods—which most people agree is false; or, one could assume that there is something special about public goods and thus, while different levels of private goods are expected, everyone should consume the same level of public goods.

To determine that everyone should consume the same level of public goods would appear to be in conflict with most individuals' preferences. Some individuals prefer to use their economic resources to obtain larger private yards rather than public parks, some want more police protection, fire protection or cleaner streets. If the same level of every good and service were provided area-wide, individuals would not be able to select a residential location with a tax/public service mix different from the average, and thus would have reduced welfare.

It is necessary, however, to distinguish between *equal* levels of public goods and services and *minimum* levels of public goods provision necessary to prevent the imposition of negative externalities on adjacent areas. If *minimum* standards are the problem, they may be dealt with through legislation by a higher political unit or adjacent units, perhaps represented by the state or federal government, might provide the economic resources for the local unit to produce a higher

[13] For example, Simon based an entire analysis on this assertion without justifying its use in *Fiscal Aspects of Metropolitan Consolidation.* See also, Jones, *Metropolitan Government,* pp. 52–72; Bollens, *The States and Metropolitan Problems,* pp. 18–19; Studenski, *Government of Metropolitan Areas,* pp. 29–30.

level of service, as is done with grant programs. Neither of these solutions to minimum standards problems requires equal service levels or a
single hierarchical political unit.

Closely related to the assertion that service levels should be equal
area-wide is the position that taxes should also be equal area-wide.[14]
If efficient use of economic resources is desired, taxes should be equal
between political jurisdictions only if identical levels of public goods
and services are provided and if costs of production are equal. If either
service levels or costs of production differ, different tax levels should
exist to reflect those differences.

Complexity of Governmental Structure
Prevents Citizen Control

A major political reform argument is that the complexity of the
political structure prevents citizens from exercising control over elected
officials and, hence, over the operation of the public economy.[15] This
is an empirical question, the theoretical aspects of which were presented
in Chapter 3. Some of the considerations here are the size of the unit—
the larger the number it contains, the less influence anyone will have;
the number of functions the unit carries out—the larger their number,
the larger the problem for citizens wanting to articulate demands on a
single issue.[16] Political reformers appear correct in their contention that
many metropolitan areas contain a larger number of units than citizens
can keep track of easily; however, one could equally well assert that a
single political unit would be too large to respond to citizens' control.
Little more than assertions in these regards exist thus far, but the
theoretical analysis in Chapter 3 does indicate the kind of questions that
must be asked to determine efficient organization of the public sector.
Evidence that the decentralization occurring in Los Angeles County,
where relatively small cities hire managers to deal with producers, may
be an efficient means toward reducing decision-making costs for articulating demand while obtaining efficient coordination was presented in

[14] Jones, *Metropolitan Government,* pp. 72–83; Simon, *Fiscal Aspects
. . . ,* pp. 7, 9; Studenski, *Government of Metropolitan Areas;* CED, *Modernizing . . . ,* p. 11.

[15] CED, *Modernizing . . . ,* pp. 11–13; Jones, *Metropolitan Government,* pp. 83–84; Bollens, *States and Metropolitan Problems,* pp. 21–22.

[16] See Ch. 3 for a discussion of this issue. Also see Gordon Tullock,
"Federalism: Problems of Scale," *Public Choice,* VI (Spring, 1969), 19–29.

Chapter 3. If anything, the recent emphasis on alienation in the United States indicates that perhaps smaller, rather than larger, political units are needed to satisfy individual preferences.[17]

Minimum Size to Achieve Economies of Scale

A minimum size (the latest estimate was 50,000 population)[18] is often specified as necessary to achieve economies of scale in production. This type of specification completely ignores the possibility of separating the unit that articulates demand from the producing unit, with the resultant recognition that different-sized units are possible for each side of the market. The *smaller* a political unit, the more likely it is that an individual can efficiently meet his own demands for public goods and services, especially if the other members have tastes for public goods and services similar to his. It is also unlikely that a minimum size can be specified as appropriate for all public goods and services, because different goods, having different characteristics, can be efficiently provided over a variety of geographic areas.

All major elements of the political reform tradition contribute to the conclusion that a single government is needed for metropolitan areas. Most of the assumptions and conclusions also strongly resemble the political science of Plato—who thought the best way to run a political system was to have a benevolent despot (Philosopher King) at the top of an administrative hierarchy. As was pointed out in Chapter 1, the benevolent-despot approach to the study of the American political system may not be appropriate because the United States constitutional structure is based on quite a different paradigm, one that focuses on the advantages of a polycentric system. In any case, the recommendations of the reform tradition do not appear consistent with an institutional structure designed to assist individuals to achieve an efficient allocation of scarce resources to meet their preferences. This may explain the conclusions drawn on political reform movements by one important political reformer, Thomas Reed:

Many better and wiser city planners and political scientists than myself have poured out millions of words, by tongue, pen and

[17] For a recent discussion of this issue, see Milton Kotler, *Neighborhood Government: The Local Foundations of Political Life* (Indianapolis: Bobbs Merrill, 1969).

[18] CED, *Modernizing Local Government*, p. 35.

typewriter, on the same theme, but frankness requires me to say that so far we have accomplished little more than the world's record for words used in proportion to cures effected.[19]

RESPONSES TO CRITIQUES OF REFORM MODELS

When the advocated reform "solution" of a single metropolitan-wide political unit has been criticized or rejected by voters, reformers have yielded to some criticisms of the reform model by proposing a federated, or two-level, structure (such as Dade County's) for the organization of the public economy in metropolitan areas.[20] The two-level structure would permit existing communities to retain control over purely local collective goods and services, while ceding control over area-wide goods and services to a metropolitan government—possibly composed of representatives of the various local communities. The problem so far apparent in this approach is obtaining agreement on just what is primarily local and what is primarily area-wide, in that the production of most public goods and services has consequences for both smaller and larger communities. One of the better analyses of the division of functions between central and local government units is Werner Hirsch's "Local versus Area-Wide Urban Government Services." [21] Hirsch delineates functions by economies of scale on the production side and by the desirability of political proximity on the demand side, then examines sources of financing in regard to the amount of income redistribution involved—that is, the greater the redistribution, the larger the political unit that provides the financing should be. However, even Hirsch neglects the possibility of separating demand articulation from production to reconcile differences between efficient demand unit and efficient production unit sizes.

While the two-level approach meets many criticisms of reform proposals, it differs from the existing situation in several ways. Com-

[19] Thomas Reed, as quoted in Norman Beckman, "Our Federal System and Urban Development: The Adaption of Form to Function," *Journal of the American Institute of Planners,* XXIX (August, 1963), 152–167.

[20] See, for example, John C. Bollens and Henry J. Schmandt, *The Metropolis* (New York: Harper & Row, 1965), ch. 15; CED, *Reshaping Government,* pp. 19–20.

[21] Werner Z. Hersch, "Local versus Area-Wide Urban Government Services," *National Tax Journal,* XVII (December, 1964), 331–339.

munities are expected to surrender veto rights on area-wide functions rather than bargain to create mutually satisfactory solutions and to prevent the imposition of political externalities. The assignment of specific functions to specific units limits opportunities to seek alternative structures for solutions to unanticipated problems because the flexibility of governmental apparatus would be restricted. One would expect that benefits from area-wide jurisdictions and reduced bargaining costs would have to greatly exceed potential political externalities before many small communities, especially those with demands diverse from the average over the entire area, would be willing to surrender their autonomy to a larger and more inclusive political unit.

However, a problem larger than one which can be solved by the pragmatic recommendation of a two-level governmental structure for metropolitan areas still exists in reform literature. It is that exceptions to the single-centered hierarchical model are viewed as *deviations* from the "ideal type" rather than as having any underlying rationale. Thus, reform theory lacks the ability to understand or predict changes in government in metropolitan areas and has no framework for undertaking empirical work to identify efficient structures for assisting individuals to meet their demands. Until these deficiencies are remedied, it is unlikely that political reform recommendations will be useful for improving governmental structure. It is unlikely that they will be accepted any more in the future than they have been in the past,[22] and where accepted, they will not improve governmental responsiveness to citizen preferences.

CONCLUSIONS

The analysis and critique of political reform assumptions and conclusions presented here is by no means the first or a complete résumé of political reform movements. Several political scientists have criticized these movements on several bases as evidenced in excellent analyses by Norton Long, Charles Adrian, and Scott Greer.[23] These scholars have

[22] Advisory Commission on Intergovernmental Relations, *Factors Affecting Voter Reactions to Governmental Reorganization in Metropolitan Areas* (Washington, D.C.: U.S. Government Printing Office, 1962).

[23] Long, "Recent Theories"; Adrian, "Metropology"; Greer, "Dilemmas of Action Research on the 'Metropolitan Problem,'" in Morris Janowitz, ed., *Community Political Systems* (Glencoe, Illinois: Free Press of Glencoe, 1961).

provided both empirical and theoretical critiques, but have not provided an alternative conceptual framework for analyzing the functioning of the state and the local public economy to take the place of the political reform model. Vincent Ostrom, Charles Tiebout, and Robert Warren provide a theoretical critique of political reform models that closely parallels the theoretical development of this study and fashions the skeleton of an alternative approach to the analysis of political systems in metropolitan areas.[24] Ostrom has related his critique of political reform to traditional political theory, while Warren has contributed a theoretical and empirical analysis of Los Angeles County, one of the more complex metropolitan areas of the United States.[25]

The time and effort devoted here to a critique of political reform movements is justified by the strength of the movements and its almost complete dominance of metropolitan political system analysis for several decades. It seems likely that recommendations for changes of metropolitan area government based on the political reform tradition will continue into the future, even though reform elements appear inconsistent with a political system dedicated to the satisfaction of individual preferences and with types of organization indicated by analysis to be the most effective means for the achievement of such preferences. The time has come to reconsider the nature of the political economy of metropolitan areas; hopefully, the framework presented in this book will hasten the uses of alternative methods of analysis to help citizens meet their demands for public goods and services—not the demands of the planners and political performers, which may be quite a different matter.

[24] Ostrom, Tiebout, and Warren, "Organization of Government."

[25] Ostrom, "Politics of Administration"; Vincent Ostrom and Elinor Ostrom, "A Behavioral Approach to the Study of Inter-Governmental Relations," *The Annals,* CCCLIX (May, 1965), 137–146; Warren, *Government in Metropolitan Regions; idem,* "A Municipal Services Market Model."

Chapter 9

CONCLUSIONS

THE PARADIGM

This study has attempted to provide a paradigm for examining the American public economy, especially the complex public economy of metropolitan areas. The paradigm uses the methodology of economics—first, the specification of assumptions (including that the basic unit of analysis is rational self-interested individuals whose resources are scarce); second, specification of empirical statements (including that many economic goods possess externalities or are public goods, that individuals possess different preferences for public as well as private goods, and that a variety of mechanisms is available to achieve coordination among individuals); and third, development of the logical implications of the assumptions and empirical statements to determine the characteristics of an efficiently structured and functioning public economy.

Following this identification of characteristics of a hypothetically efficient public economy, an examination of the American public economy was undertaken by analysis of (1) the general structure and coordinating mechanisms used in the public sector, (2) the actual metropolitan area public economies of Dade County and Los Angeles County, (3) the functional areas of education and air pollution control, and (4) income redistribution in a federal system. Each of these examinations led to a conclusion that the paradigm did provide an explanatory mechanism and was of considerable usefulness in understanding the structure and functioning of the American public economy. Interpretations of the American public economy developed in the study differ in important respects from those reached by the metropolitan political reform tradition. These differences have been explored to indicate some of the problems arising from that tradition and some probable reasons for the failure of political reform recommendations to gain acceptance from citizens in the United States.

SOME NORMATIVE IMPLICATIONS

Normative implications can be drawn from this and other studies based on similar paradigms if one agrees that (1) the positive analysis is useful and (2) the economy and polity should be organized to meet individual preferences as perceived by the individuals who make up the society. The case for the usefulness of positive analysis rests on this and similar studies. The case for primacy of individual preferences in evaluating the consequences of alternative social, political, and economic institutions is an ethical one.

Economics and economic approaches are often criticized as being based on acceptance of the idea that man is essentially selfish, whereas man *should* really be selfless and act as his brother's keeper. One often hears "competition" should be replaced by "cooperation" as the ethic upon which society's organization should be based. One can, however, interpret economic approaches to the study of social interaction in quite a different manner. Since economics focuses on voluntary agreements between and among individuals for mutual benefit, it is essentially a study of cooperation between individuals—where each individual takes action from which the other party receives benefits. Competition is an essential part of this system, with competing options setting the boundaries for cooperative interaction as each competitor strives to provide *more* benefits for individuals with whom he enters into exchange relationships, and with each exchange relationship ultimately depending on the cooperation of the parties involved. An economy based on voluntary cooperation, rather than on central direction, would appear to approach the ultimate of a society of individuals "do[ing] unto others as you would have them do unto you."

The extension of this principle to large-group action through the creation of political organizations permits men to achieve higher levels of well-being than would otherwise be possible while still maintaining the primacy of individual preferences. It is also likely that greater satisfaction will be achieved in a society in which men are constantly aware of gains that can be made through voluntary agreements and are encouraged to seek solutions to problems in such a manner that everyone gains, as opposed to a society in which cooperation is viewed as a process by which one person gains at the expense of another.

As the economy and polity become increasingly complex, it appears even more important that we understand how coordination takes place in a decentralized polycentric polity in order that higher levels of knowledge can be developed to solve problems and to advance human well-being without seeking an omniscient central authority. Such an authority would lack the capability of identifying individual preferences for an efficient allocation of resources and, therefore, would ultimately tend to resort to despotic solutions—subverting the preferences of individual citizens to the preferences of the planners controlling the centralized mechanism.

The paradigm presented in this study, which provides a method for analyzing complex economic and political systems, would appear to be an important advance over those that simply describe decentralized polities as chaotic and recommend, in their place, a despotic solution.

SELECTED BIBLIOGRAPHY

Advisory Commission on Intergovernmental Relations. *Fiscal Balance in the American Federal System*. Washington, D.C.: U.S. Government Printing Office, 1967.

———. *The Problem of Special Districts in American Government*. Washington, D.C.: U.S. Government Printing Office, 1964.

Alchian, Armen A. "Uncertainty, Evolution and Economic Theory." *Journal of Political Economy,* LVIII (June, 1950): 211–221.

Barzel, Yoram. "Two Propositions on the Optimum Level of Producing Collective Goods." *Public Choice,* VI (Spring, 1969): 31–37.

Baumol, William J. *Welfare Economics and the Theory of the State*. Cambridge, Mass.: Harvard University Press, 1965.

Booms, Bernard H., and Ward, James E., Jr. "The Cons of Black Capitalism." *Business Horizons,* VII (October, 1969): 17–26.

Bowen, William H. "The Interpretation of Voting and the Allocation of Economic Resources." *Quarterly Journal of Economics,* LVIII (November, 1943): 27–48.

Braybrooke, David, and Lindblom, Charles E. *A Strategy of Decision*. New York: Free Press, 1963.

Buchanan, James M. *Fiscal Theory and Political Economy*. Chapel Hill: University of North Carolina Press, 1960.

Buchanan, James M., and Stubblebine, William Craig. "Externality." *Economica,* N.S. XXIX (November, 1962): 371–384.

Buchanan, James M., and Tullock, Gordon. *The Calculus of Consent*. Ann Arbor: University of Michigan Press, 1962.

Burkhead, Jesse. *Input and Output in Large-City High Schools*. Syracuse, N.Y.: Syracuse University Press, 1967.

Coase, Ronald H. "The Problem of Social Cost." *The Journal of Law and Economics,* XXX (October, 1960): 1–44.

Committee for Economic Development. *Modernizing Local Government*. New York: Committee for Economic Development, 1966.

Dahl, Robert A., and Lindblom, Charles E. *Politics, Economics and Welfare*. New York: Harper & Row, 1953.

Demsetz, Harold. "Why Regulate Utilities?" *Journal of Law and Economics,* XI (April, 1968): 55–65.

Downs, Anthony. *An Economic Theory of Democracy.* New York: Harper & Row, 1957.

——. *Urban Problems and Prospects.* Chicago: Markham, 1970.

——. "Competition and Community Schools." In Henry M. Levin, ed., *Community Control of Schools.* Washington, D.C.: Brookings, 1970.

Friedman, Milton. "The Role of Government in Education." In Robert A. Solow, ed., *Economics and the Public Interest.* New Brunswick, N.J.: Rutgers University Press, 1955.

Gittell, Marilyn, ed. *Educating an Urban Population.* Beverley Hills, Calif.: Sage, 1967.

Gittell, Marilyn, and Hollander, T. Edward. *Six Urban School Districts.* New York: Praeger, 1968.

Grodzins, Morton. *The American System.* Chicago: Rand McNally, 1966.

Hamilton, Alexander, Jay, John, and Madison, James. *The Federalist.* New York: Modern Library, n.d.

Hayek, F. A. "The Use of Knowledge in Society." *American Economic Review,* XXXV (September, 1945): 519–530.

Hirsch, Werner Z. "Local versus Area-Wide Urban Government Services." *National Tax Journal,* XVII (December, 1964): 331–339.

——. "The Supply of Urban Public Services." In Harvey S. Perloff and Lowden Wingo, Jr., eds., *Issues in Urban Economics.* Baltimore: Johns Hopkins Press, 1968.

Hirsch, Werner Z., Segelhorst, Elbert W., and Marcus, Morton J. *Spill-over of Public Education Costs and Benefits.* Los Angeles: University of California, Institute of Government and Public Affairs, 1964.

Kotler, Milton. *Neighborhood Government: The Local Foundations of Political Life.* Indianapolis: Bobbs Merrill, 1969.

Law and Contemporary Problems, XXXIII (Spring, 1968). (Issue on Air Pollution Control.)

Lindblom, Charles E. *The Intelligence of Democracy.* New York: Free Press, 1965.

Long, Norton E. "Recent Theories and Problems of Local Government." Pp. 285–95 in Carl J. Friedrich and Seymour E. Harris, eds., *Public Policy,* VIII, Cambridge, Mass.: Graduate School of Public Administration, Harvard University, 1958.

Maxey, Chester. "The Political Integration of Metropolitan Communities." *National Municipal Review,* XI (August, 1922): 229–253.

McKean, Roland N. "The Unseen Hand in Government." *American Economic Review,* LV (June, 1965): 496–506.

Mitchell, William C. "The Shape of Political Theory to Come: From Political Sociology to Political Economy." *American Behavioral Scientist,* XI (November–December, 1967), 8–37.

———. *Public Choice in America: An Introduction to American Government.* Chicago: Markham, 1971.

Moses, Leon and Williamson, Harold F., Jr. "The Location of Economic Activity in Cities." *American Economic Review,* LVII (May, 1967): 211–222.

Musgrave, Richard A. *The Theory of Public Finance.* New York: McGraw-Hill, 1959.

Musgrave, Richard A., and Peacock, Alan T., eds. *Classics in the Theory of Public Finance.* New York: St. Martin's Press, 1967.

Mushkin, Selma J., and Cotton, John F. *Sharing Federal Funds for State and Local Needs.* New York: Praeger, 1969.

Olson, Mancur, Jr. *The Logic of Collective Action: Public Goods and the Theory of Groups.* Cambridge, Mass.: Harvard University Press, 1965.

Ostrom, Elinor. "On the Variety of Potential Public Goods." Mimeographed. Bloomington, Ind.: Indiana University.

Ostrom, Vincent. "Operational Federalism: Organization for the Provision of Public Services in the American Federal System." *Public Choice,* VII (Spring, 1969): 1–17.

———. "The Political Theory of the Compound Republic: An Essay on the Federalist Papers." Mimeographed. Bloomington, Ind.: Department of Government, Indiana University, 1969.

———. "Water Resource Development: Some Problems in Economic and Political Analysis of Public Policy." Pp. 123–150 in Austin Ranney, ed., *Political Science and Public Policy.* Chicago: Markham, 1968.

———. "The Politics of Administration." Mimeographed. Bloomington, Ind.: Department of Government, Indiana University.

Ostrom, Vincent, and Ostrom, Elinor. "A Behavioral Approach to the Study of Inter-Governmental Relations." *The Annals,* CCCLIX (May, 1965): 137–146.

Ostrom, Vincent, Tiebout, Charles, and Warren, Robert, "The Organization of Government in Metropolitan Areas: A Theoretical

Inquiry." *American Political Science Review,* LV (December, 1961): 831–842.

Samuelson, Paul. "Diagrammatic Exposition of a Theory of Public Expenditure." *Review of Economics and Statistics,* XXXVII (November, 1955): 350–356.

Sofen, Edward. *Miami Metropolitan Experiment.* Bloomington, Ind.: Indiana University Press, 1963.

Tax Foundation. *Tax Burdens and Benefits of Government Expenditures by Income Class, 1961 and 1965,* New York: Tax Foundation, 1967.

Tiebout, Charles M. "A Pure Theory of Local Expenditures." *Journal of Political Economy,* LXIV (October, 1956): 416–424.

Tullock, Gordon. "Federalism: Problems of Scale." *Public Choice,* VI (Spring, 1969): 19–29.

———. *The Politics of Bureaucracy.* Washington, D.C.: Public Affairs Press, 1965.

Wagner, Richard E. "Pressure Groups and Political Entrepreneurs." Pp. 161–170 in Gordon Tullock, ed., *Papers on Non-market Decision Making.* Charlottesville, Va.: Thomas Jefferson Center for Political Economy, 1966.

Waldo, Dwight. *The Administrative State.* New York: Roland Press, 1948.

Warren, Robert O. "A Municipal Services Market Model of Metropolitan Organization." *Journal of the American Institute of Planners,* XXX (August, 1964): 193–204.

———. *Government in Metropolitan Regions: A Reappraisal of Fractionated Political Organization.* Davis, Calif.: Institute of Governmental Affairs, University of California, 1966.

Wildavsky, Aaron. *The Politics of the Budgetary Process.* Boston and Toronto: Little, Brown, 1964.

Williamson, Oliver. "Hierarchical Control and Optimum Firm Size." *Journal of Political Economy,* LXXV (April, 1967): 123–138.

Wolff, Reinhold. *Miami Metro.* Coral Gables, Fla.: University of Miami, Bureau of Business and Economic Research, 1960.

Wood, Thomas J. "Dade County: Unbossed, Erratically Led." *The Annals,* CCCLIII (May, 1964): 64–71.

INDEX